Dogs

John Gordon

S0-CCJ-345

John Bartholomew & Son Limited
Edinburgh and London

Contents

First published in Great Britain 1976 *by*
JOHN BARTHOLOMEW & SON LIMITED
12 Duncan Street, Edinburgh EH9 1TA
And at 216 High Street, Bromley BR1 1PW

ISBN 0 7028 1023 1

1st edition

Designed and illustrated by Allard Design Group Limited
Printed in Great Britain by W. S. Cowell Limited, Ipswich, Suffolk

Pointer

Poodle

Alsatian (German Shepherd)

GREYHOUNDS	HOUNDS	GUN DOGS		GUARD DOGS
Afghan	Basset	Bloodhound	Labrador	Boxer
Borzoi	Beagle	Cocker Spaniel	Norfolk Spaniel	Doberman
English Greyhound	Bloodhound	English Setter	Pointer	Great Dane
Irish Wolfhound	Foxhound	German Pointer	Springer Spaniel	Newfoundland
Saluki		Golden Retriever	Weimeraner	St. Bernard
Whippet		Irish Setter		

HUNTING DOGS

SHEPHERD DOGS	TERRIERS		PET DOGS	
Alsatian	Airedale Terrier	Daschund	Bulldog	Pug
Collie	Bedlington Terrier	Scottish Terrier	Chihuahua	Schipperke
Old English Shepherd Dog	Boston Terrier	Smooth-haired Terrier	Dalmatian	Yorkshire Terrier
Pyrenean Mountain Dog	Bull Terrier	Staffordshire Bull Terrier	Pekingese	
Shetland Sheep Dog	Cairn Terrier	West Highland White Terrier	Pomeranian	
	Corgi	Wire-haired Fox Terrier	Poodle	

WORKING DOGS   **PET DOGS**

Choice of breed

Picking the 'right' puppy

Pedigree dogs have the advantage over mongrels in that they have known standards of physical uniformity as well as in-built disposition and character. These standards have been bred into their bloodlines, often for centuries, to suit that particular breed's working requirements. Thus, a Corgi (you know roughly what size it will be) is swift, sharp, and dashing because it was bred to 'heel' and herd cattle by nipping them behind to make them move! If you want a big, formidable guard dog you may go for a German Shepherd or an Irish Wolfhound; if you do, then you know your food bills are going to be high. On the other hand, if you buy a mongrel puppy you may have no idea how it will turn out, either in size or character, as you have no guide to its ancestry. It may prove too big, too hairy, too slinky for your fancy or your needs. But if you want just a nice companion with no pedigree to boast about, then it might be perfect!

Some breeds lend themselves to a happy outdoor kennel life, whereas other less-hardy breeds or varieties would soon succumb if kept out of doors. Others are adaptable to flat life or have been bred to work and please the sportsman. You must remember the exercise needed by certain varieties – it is not much use choosing one of these if you cannot regularly walk the dog. Confined living suits some of the Toy breeds, but what would satisfy a Pekingese would probably reduce a big working Collie to abject misery. Some breeds, though, in spite of their pastoral leanings, can be brought up to enjoy town and family life.

Consideration must be given to your new dog's future size. Big dogs cost a good deal to feed, especially these days when fresh raw meat is so highly priced; you will not get away by feeding him family left-overs. A dog needs to be kept in good condition and good food and enough exercise are two important factors towards this end. It is not fair on a big dog to take him into your home if he is not to be fed amply and well. He will soon decline in health and vigour, may well cost a good deal in veterinary bills and prove a misery to himself and a worry to his owner.

Grooming is another thing to think about. A Poodle or a Fox Terrier (Wire), are just two of several breeds which require regular trimming and grooming. An un-trimmed Poodle looks terrible, often indistinguishable from a mongrel in appearance, and does little or nothing to recommend his breed.

There are other considerations involved when buying a particular breed. A family with very small children should avoid introducing a small breed to the home. A Yorkshire Terrier, or another very tiny dog, such as a Pomeranian, cannot sustain too much pulling about and squeezing. These breeds have too frail a body structure to allow children to play with them boisterously – however well-meaning such play may be. People living in the country on un-fenced land must consider proper kennelling or the sporting dog they buy, say, the Beagle or Basset Hound, will be out and away in the far-off fields. The woman about to present her husband with an addition to their family would be ill-advised to buy an excitable breed like a Staffordshire Bull Terrier, capable of directing himself like a missile at her middle. On the other hand, this breed would probably make a wonderful nursemaid for the toddler.

The following table will give the reader a rough guide to the suitability of certain breeds in the home, although one has to bear in mind that temperament plays a part in the individual animal. The breeds have been put in groups and in popularity order, according to Kennel Club comparitive tables of registrations for 1974.

Prospective owners should ensure that no dog is left alone in the home for lengthy periods and that he has access at all times to fresh drinking water. Remember, too, that a lonely dog will bark, whine, and often prove destructive in his urge to while away the time. One has a certain duty to neighbours and they should not have a noisy dog inflicted upon them for hours at a time. A dog so treated may well become nervous and develop unreliable tendencies, quite apart from proving extremely difficult to train or maintain in house cleanliness.

Dog or bitch?

Some owners prefer the male of the species because of its naturally more positive and aggressive attitude. Others favour the bitch, believing that she is sweeter and, having an inherent tendency to guard the 'nest', will make a better guard. Sometimes this prefer-ence is qualified by the fact that they believe the bitch with her periods of 'heat', which occur normally at no less than six-monthly intervals and last up to three weeks, can prove a nuisance in the home. Admittedly, this is a point which has dissuaded many people from choosing a bitch. But the problem – if indeed it is one – can be dealt with by treating a bitch in season with one of

Hounds group:	Size	Exercise	Grooming	Flat	House	Fa
Afghan Hound	Large	Plenty	Plenty		x	
Beagle	Small	Moderate	Not much	x	x	x
Dachshund	Small	Little	Little	x	x	x
Basset Hound	Medium	Moderate	Not much		x	x
Whippet	Small	Moderate	Not much	x	x	x
Gundog group:						
Labrador Retriever	Large	Plenty	Moderate		x	x
Spaniel (various)	Medium	Moderate	Plenty	x	x	
Golden Retriever	Large	Plenty	Moderate		x	
Irish Setter	Medium	Plenty	Moderate		x	
German Shorthaired Pointer	Large	Plenty	Moderate		x	x
Terriers:						
West Highland White	Small	Moderate	Moderate	x	x	x
Cairn	Small	Moderate	Moderate	x	x	x
Staffordshire Bull	Medium	Plenty	Not much		x	x
Scottish	Small	Moderate	Moderate	x	x	x
Utility group:						
Poodle (Toy)	Small	Moderate	Plenty	x	x	
Poodle (Miniature)	Small	Moderate	Plenty	x	x	
Dalmation	Large	Plenty	Moderate		x	
Chow Chow	Large	Moderate	Plenty		x	
Shih Tzu	Small	Moderate	Plenty	x	x	
Working group:						
German Shepherd Dog (Alsatian)	Large	Plenty	Moderate		x	x
Collie (Rough)	Large	Plenty	Moderate		x	x
Shetland Sheepdog	Medium	Moderate	Plenty	x	x	
Old English Sheepdog	Large	Plenty	Plenty			x
Boxer	Large	Plenty	Not much		x	x
Toy group:						
Yorkshire Terrier	Small	Moderate	Plenty	x	x	
Cavalier King Charles Spaniel	Small	Moderate	Plenty	x	x	
Pekingese	Small	Moderate	Plenty	x	x	
Chihuahua	Small	Moderate	Not much	x	x	
Pomeranian	Small	Moderate	Plenty	x	x	

the excellent preparations now available to dog-owners. Some take the form of tinctures or oils, which when rubbed into the coat of the bitch's hindquarters will screen her sexual scent from unwanted suitors, at least to some extent. Probably more effective is a product of chlorophyll which, when administered orally in tablet form just prior to the vital time when the bitch is expected to be ready for mating, will effectively deodorise her rear end. With such aids she can be exercised even out of doors during her heat, providing she is kept on a lead and carried a distance from and to her front doorstep. This little manoeuvre should serve to hoodwink all but the most persistent admirers. A bitch is usually rather easier to train than a dog, and apart from her times of season, she is less inclined to wander, or to fight. It is not necessary to allow her a litter if her having a family should prove inconvenient to you: her life will not be shortened, neither need she have any physical disorders in later life, as some seem to think. In fact, many un-mated bitches have exceeded the life span that might have been expected of them. On the other hand, a male dog which has never been allowed to mate may well prove an unhappy animal, wanting to wander off and search for bitches. Such a dog frustrated in his desires can prove an embarrassment indoors and become soured in his disposition. A remedy in such a case is to have the dog castrated, which is a simple enough if rather drastic veterinary operation. Bitches can be dealt with in a similar manner – this is called 'spaying', the surgical removal of the ovaries. Both operations should be done (only if absolutely necessary) as early as possible in the animal's life. Dogs neutered in this manner may incline towards fatness, glossiness, and laziness, although expert opinions have been held to the contrary. A point that should be understood, though, is that no castrated dog or spayed bitch is eligible for exhibition according to Kennel Club rules and regulations.

How much will it cost?

The cost of a puppy can vary from a nominal price for a cross-bred or mongrel to quite a substantial sum for an Irish Wolfhound or some rare and unusual breed. As the cost of foodstuffs continues to rise so alarmingly, the trend may well be towards smaller dogs and they could well prove more expensive to buy than their big brothers. Price can be ascertained only when you come to buy one, as market values fluctuate with popularity and/or scarcity. Whatever you have to pay initially, it will be nothing compared with what it will cost you to feed and maintain the dog, assuming he lives his normal life span. Then follows the cost of inoculations, equipment, and dog licence fees. No doubt in sickness the animal will require veterinary attention which is a considerable expense these days. If you have chosen a breed such as a Poodle, there is the cost of trimming to consider and this would of necessity be a regular outgoing. If you go abroad for your holidays the dog will need to be kennelled out while you are away. Many people insure their dogs against loss and theft, and cover for personal liability; if a bitch, insurance against whelping problems is sometimes sought. All such things cost money, although most owners think it is worth it all to have a smart, pleasing, and loyal companion; and no doubt it is.

Where to buy

Most breeds will be found advertised in the weekly canine journals. Generally speaking, a breeder is better to buy from than a dealer. The former breeds his own stock and specialises in that breed, whereas a dealer buys in stock to re-sell. This does not mean that you might not get a good one from a dealer. If he is selective in what he buys and knows his subject he will make sure that he handles only the typical and sound puppies, whereas a

Afghan Hound

breeder with a litter of puppies may well be obliged to sell the lot however varied their quality. Always take time to shop around before buying. Go to several kennels and see what they have got. Ask questions and learn from the answers. If you have made up your mind which breed you fancy, learn something about that breed before you start. Most breeds have had their own little handbooks published and in such a book you will find the official breed Standard telling you what physical features to look for. It will also tell you something of that breed's origin and history, its disposition, and how to feed and maintain it in good health and happiness. The breeder himself is usually only too willing to help and advise you and show you his stock, for invariably he is an enthusiast. If you buy from him he will probably present you with a feeding, welfare, and maintenance chart as a guide to the early stages of ownership. He will also tell you what inoculations are, or will be, needed.

Always insist on the right to have your new puppy examined and passed as sound and healthy by a veterinary surgeon. Few breeders will object to this proviso, subject of course to your paying the professional's bill. Health and soundness are of vital importance and worth more than cuteness and appearance, although you are entitled to all these things with correct breed character if you buy an expensive pedigree puppy.

Basset Hound

Is pedigree important?

Yes it is, but there is a true saying that no dog is worth any more than his pedigree, provided the pedigree is true. Further, no pedigree is worth any more than the dog himself. To explain this, you cannot boast about your Cocker Spaniel having a wonderful pedigree if your Cocker Spaniel is a poor specimen of his breed. Similarly, if you have a beautiful specimen, admired by all and his pedigree is poor – all his ancestry being shabby specimens – he is unlikely to produce anything good in his sons and daughters. In effect, his offspring will be no better than his pedigree. The ideal animal to own is a good one from good breeding.

Soundness

This, of course, is a prime consideration when buying your dog. For the pet owner particularly, it means that in having a sound dog he has one which is near enough coordinately perfect in its skeletal make-up, its constitution, and temperament. It means that his dog is likely to give minimal trouble in the way of health and will not be vicious and untenable. In the case of a pedigree dog of a specific breed, that dog will possess true breed character. One who does not can be rightly termed unsound.

Gun Dogs

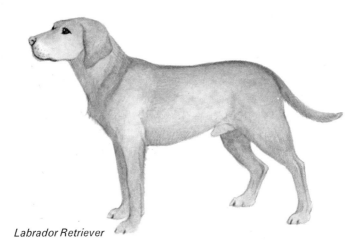

Labrador Retriever

It should be realised that unsoundness can be inherited or acquired. A dog affected by genetic weaknesses will pass on these faults to his progeny – that is why it is useful, when buying a puppy, to obtain at least a glance at its parents. *Acquired* unsoundness may come from faulty rearing or with a dog brought up in a deprived environment. A dog so affected should not pass on such flaws to his offspring, if any.

As a general rule, anything in a dog's make-up which impairs his usefulness, whether this be permanent or temporary, can be regarded as an unsoundness. It can apply to a dog who is below par in health, in his working ability, or in his action and movement. For the pet owner good character and disposition in his dog is vital and anyone contemplating the purchase of an unsound dog or one suspected of unsoundness should examine most carefully that dog's history and his nature.

Type

Type is rather difficult to define. In dog parlance it mainly concerns distinct pedigree breeds. All such breeds have their standards of excellence and these are laid down by their expert governing bodies and approved by the Kennel Club (similar bodies exist in most countries). They describe what is believed to be the perfect

Springer Spaniel

specimen of their kind. Breeders breed to this 'model' or ideal dog; judges judge to it. Type plays an important part in the dog and whereas a pedigree dog *must* have type, even though this is not and cannot be written into breed standards, a mongrel or cross-bred dog may carry only a fleeting glimpse of a type inherited from some breed way back in his ancestry. Thus, we have breed type which depends largely on a dog's anatomical structure and general appearance whereas individual type is expressed more by points and detail. A typey dog stands out, as a rule, against a dog lacking type. Very broadly speaking, you may liken it to physical and temperamental personality in humans which causes one person to stand out from his fellows.

Veterinary examination

No reputable breeder or dealer is likely to object to your having a puppy's health checked and the animal confirmed sound and fit by a qualified veterinary surgeon before you buy it. Naturally, the cost of this examination must be born by yourself, but to many whose knowledge of dogflesh is scant, the nominal fee outlay will be considered well worthwhile. The veterinary surgeon will advise also on immunisation and tell you what vaccination programme to follow in order to safeguard your puppy's health.

Scottish Terrier

Cairn Terrier

Kennel-club registration

Most people buying a pedigree dog will wish to register their puppy at the kennel club of their country: most countries have kennel clubs. When you purchased your puppy you should have been given either a registration certificate or a partially completed registration application form. If the former, it will indicate that the dog is already registered with a name by the breeder or previous owner. Then you will need to do no more than to transfer the ownership of that name to yourself. In most countries there is a special form – a transfer form – for that purpose and a nominal fee is usually required. If you have to register the dog with a name, you complete the registration application form with a suitable name and submit it to the kennel club with the appropriate fee. So many names are already taken that you may wish to list two or three alternatives and leave the kennel club to make the final choice for you. Registered names are in themselves not particularly important and may not necessarily bear any relation to the dog's pet name. But a choice of name is worth some thought: if the dog is to be exhibited later on and proves successful in the show-ring, his name will be recorded and maybe talked about if he proves a top-flight specimen. Should this be so then it is worth evolving a suitable and perhaps imposing name for him. It should be noted that no dog can be exhibited at any official show unless he has been properly registered.

When purchasing a dog a registration certificate or partially completed registration form should be received from the previous owner.

The puppy arrives home

Kennel or the home?

This is a question asked by most new dog owners. Much depends, of course, for what purpose you have bought the dog. If he is to be a guard dog, purely and simply, and meant to keep an eye and ear on business premises, then he has to be accommodated either in or adjacent to the property itself. This might mean a kennel, although a guard dog normally functions better if he is confined within the walls of his domain. If he is kept outside it, he can be sidetracked too easily by intruders and rendered less effective. If he has to be kennelled, then make sure that his home is a comfortable one. The dog should be able to lie out with his legs fully extended. Standing up in comfort, he should be able to turn round without trouble. The entrance to the kennel should be protected against the elements to screen him from driving rain and debilitating draughts. A piece of carpeting or hessian strong and heavy enough to flap down over the doorway without hindering his comings and goings would be ideal. For ventilation, a chimney cowl system is the best plan and this can be adapted simply enough to the roof of the average kennel.

Kennels should be constructed on dry, well-drained ground. Concrete is generally satisfactory, but a concrete base upon which the kennel is raised with blocks to allow under-floor ventilation is better. Ordinary bricks are useful for making bases, but, being porous, bricks absorb odours: solid concrete blocks are preferable. An excellent base is asphalt. This can be washed down and swilled with disinfectant and be scrubbed *ad infinitum*. It is generally the most hygienic of floors for a kennel. Make sure that the ground upon which the kennel is built slopes gently to a drain. The area should be washed over at least once a day to maintain effective hygiene. Face the kennel door south, ensuring that it does not lie beneath trees which drip water in bad weather. The dog should be able to retire to a shady spot in the height of summer. No dog will thrive in the scorching sun any more than he will in bitter winter weather in an unprotected position.

The kennel roof and sides should be thoroughly insulated from the wet: there are plenty of proprietary lining and roofing materials available. Inside the kennel make the animal comfortable, and, most important, the dog must be dry. If he sleeps in damp surroundings he will soon suffer in health. Woodwool is probably the driest and best medium for bedding down a dog and keeping him warm and fit. If you can arrange the kennel in such a way that it is built with a sliding bench raised a few inches above floor level, this will be found an ideal arrangement: cleaning-out time will be reduced to a minimum. Strict hygiene is of vital importance if a guard dog is to thrive and do his job well. Make sure the whole kennel area is well scrubbed down with a suitable disinfectant.

It is never a good idea to chain a kennel dog. He will rub the chain against his coat and this may well cause body sores. Quite apart from this his morale will be affected: chained dogs have been known to prove unreliable even to their owners. If you must use a chain employ linkage which has spring hooks and about two swivels distributed down its length. This will prevent the chain winding around the dog's neck.

The best way to employ a guard dog on business premises is to let it loose in the building or enclosed area to be guarded. Place the dog's bed in a reasonably warm, dry, and draughtproof corner or install an old armchair upon which he can jump and curl up. He will appreciate this and it will not impair his sense of duty. With the whole place to patrol he can give an alarm if necessary at any given point. During daytime he can be kept outside in a suitable kennel, preferably one which has a chain link

A 'tailor-made' kennel

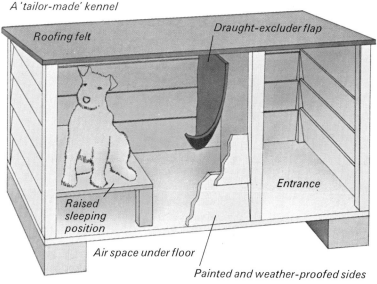

Roofing felt

Draught-excluder flap

Entrance

Raised sleeping position

Air space under floor

Painted and weather-proofed sides

run. Alternatively, he can be linked by chain and ring to a strong wire or metal rod spanned between two trees or points so that he has a free run between them yet cannot wander into an operative area without warning.

Kennels ideal for show dogs are necessarily plusher. The average small show kennel keeps a minimum of four dogs. These are bedded down separately and it is best to have wired runs linked to each kennel so that its occupant can be let out at will to exercise. Any extension of such a kennel depends largely upon your ambitions and your pocketbook. There are plenty of well-designed kennels available on the market today: all the big prefabricated-kennel makers offer an excellent selection. Make certain that you have a small kennel separate from the rest to be used as an isolation home for a sick dog. A small adjoining cupboard space where fresh bedding, a bucket and pail, and kennel equipment can be stored is a worthwhile idea. Surround the range entirely with chain-link fencing and depending upon your breed make sure this is high enough to prevent jumpers from escaping, which means an average height of at least six feet. Choose the site with care — it needs to be free from prevailing winds and open enough to allow plenty of sunshine to filter through. A south or south-west aspect is excellent, and kennels which stand on well-drained, gravelly soil are usually easy to maintain and offer good health advantages to the occupants. A site which is bordered by trees can prove shady, but overhanging and brushing foliage is often a nuisance when the days are windy. Try to site the kennels in a place where the trees can provide shade when necessary but not drip too much in the wet season.

Treat the kennel woodwork with a suitable preservative. There are a number of good sorts available which are harmless to dogs. Kennel floors should be raised from ground level by short concrete pillars about nine inches high. The space so made should be surrounded with fine-mesh wire netting to prevent cats and vermin entering beneath, fouling the ground, and annoying the dogs. Sawdust should be brushed out when soiled, and a daily cleansing and disinfecting is essential for the maintenance of hygiene.

Indoor kennels are usually for the small or Toy dogs: a wide range is available for the dog market. They are suited to spare rooms, conservatories, or even outhouses, and can accommodate half a dozen dogs or more within a small space. They are extremely useful when a number of dogs are involved around the house. Remember that when you have two or more dogs running together

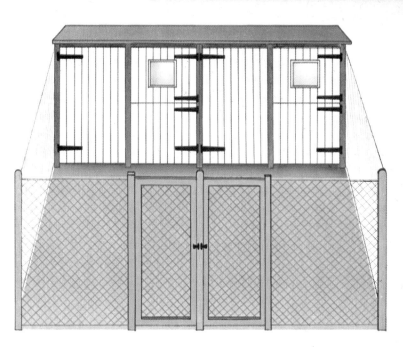

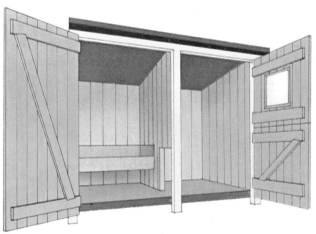

Kennels for show dogs are plusher than ordinary outdoor kennels.

you have the nucleus of a pack, with all the mischief that a pack can get up to ! It is useful to be able to tuck them away nice and quietly when you want to, and with small dogs such indoor kennels are invaluable. Even the small breeds need to be seen and not heard at times, although to achieve both happy states is more a matter of training : dogs which have been suddenly kennelled against their will can often prove most vociferous ! If you really intend to expand in the Toy-dog-breeding field, indoor kennels of the sort described can be kept 'everywhere' about the house – in rooms, under the sink and stairs, and in fact anywhere where space and family opinion permits.

Dogs are generally best kept indoors. There they become a member of the family circle – they learn what is wanted of them, how to behave, and how to prove effective and sharp watchdogs. Kept in a kennel for most of the day, a dog becomes dull, often dispirited, and suffers mentally because he lacks the human company which most dogs thrive on. It will be found that the average dog is anxious to please his owner, to learn his every whim and to *enjoy* pleasing him.

Some dogs bed down well in a basket, but this is better for the adult rather than the small puppy who will chew and gnaw at

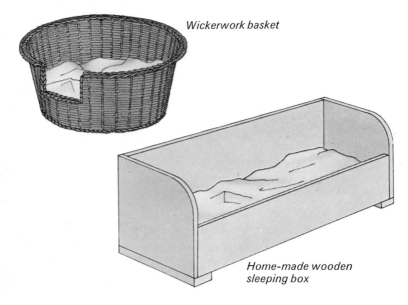

Wickerwork basket

Home-made wooden sleeping box

wickerwork during his teething period. This is why the purchase of a basket should be deferred at least until a dog has his second or permanent teeth. The ideal sleeping accommodation for the one dog is an open box, made to suit the size of the breed. It should be an open-top oblong box with sides sufficiently high to allow the dog entry and to protect him snugly against draughts. If the animal is particularly small, a doorway can be cut in one side to allow his entry and departure. The base should be lined with a loose warm blanket which can be shaken out daily and replaced at regular intervals. As the dog grows the box can be increased in size or replaced with a commercial dog bed.

Home cleanliness

No one can expect a small puppy coming fresh from the breeder to be at once clean around the home. Even had he shown some promise in this direction while still with his mother, the entirely new geography of your home would certainly confuse him initially. Some owners show a greater aptitude at teaching dogs than do others – some have more time to expend than others. These points and the fact that some breeds learn quicker than others, causes the period of graduation in home cleanliness to vary. Much, too, will depend on a puppy's early environment; a youngster which has been left untrained and allowed to pick and choose his own time and place for his motions is capable of forming dirty habits which you may find extremely difficult to eradicate. This is why time *must* be found and considerable patience used in order to make the new member of the family clean in his habits as soon as possible.

It should be remembered (and this is a useful rule) that once a sleeping puppy awakes he will want to urinate. Do *not* watch him open his eyes, take a lengthy stretch, walk around for ten seconds, then squat and make a puddle on your best carpet! Pick him up *before* he goes through all these exercises, take him to his sand or dirt tray (if you have a flat) or into the garden (if you have a house). Say some word of command such as 'Tray', 'Garden', or 'Out', or some suitable monosyllabic word, which you must keep using during training. Keep him there until he has relieved himself. After a while, with your help, watchfulness, and guidance he will make for the tray or garden door as soon as he wakes up. If he cannot reach the objective because you are not there to open doors or navigate him and he has an 'accident', then do not blame or scold him. Gradually, he will learn what is expected of him and you will have a properly house-trained puppy. *Never* rub his nose into any mess he makes. This is unfair. Show it to him at close quarters by all means, scolding him meanwhile – there is no harm in doing this, and he will sense your displeasure. Clean up thoroughly after such incidents and sprinkle the spot with a disinfectant: this will erase the scent which if allowed to remain will draw the puppy back to the scene to do it again. Some owners use pepper deterrent instead of disinfectant, but this is not recommended in puppy training. Never thrash a dog; this will do nothing but destroy his confidence in you and it may well make him a nervous animal and impossible to train.

If you propose to keep your puppy in the kitchen at night, you have a choice of two good and tried methods. One is to bed him down in a tea chest open end upwards so that he cannot get out. The floor of the box should be well lined with newspapers so that his overnight messes are confined to a relatively small area and can be easily and quickly lifted out in the morning and disposed of. Alternatively, you can lay down newspapers all over the kitchen floor before you retire. Then when you enter the kitchen in the morning, any soiled newspapers can be speedily scooped up and destroyed, the puppy being put out at once into

To house-train a puppy take him to his sand or dirt tray whenever he shows signs of wanting to relieve himself and say the word 'TRAY' each time.

the garden. Most youngsters, however well trained they may seem during daylight hours, will have lapses overnight. This is due largely to the fact that they have limited muscular control over their bladder and bowels. As they grow this control improves and this fact plus the effect of their training quickly makes for an ability to 'hold' themselves during the night and attend to their motions immediately upon being put into the garden.

Intelligent aid by an owner is important in this house-training exercise. It is wise not to put down milk or allow the puppy any drink or food just before retiring. Let him wander about in the garden for a while before you bed him down for the night and never delay putting him out first thing in the morning. He will hear you moving around as soon as you rise and will leave his box or basket in anticipation of greeting you. He may well have been clean all night, but once on his feet will probably disgrace himself even a few moments before you get to him. This is why with small puppies it is a good idea to go straight to them in the morning and put them outside. Remember, too, that meat produces considerably less excrement than bread, apart from being better for the average dog's health and development.

Dew claws

These are the rudimentary fifth claws to be found on the insides of a dog's forelegs and sometimes on the hindlegs too. They grow a little up from the rest of the toes and although likened to the thumb in humans, they appear to serve no useful purpose in the dog.

Most pedigree breeds experts are adamant on the point that dew claws on *hind* legs *must* be removed. The majority of breeds remove the dew claws on the forelegs automatically within a short time of a puppy's birth. If you own a puppy of a specific breed it is advisable to check with a knowledgeable breeder as to what you should do, as for example the Pyrenian Mountain Dog should have double dew claws on its back legs. Certainly, dew claws can prove a nuisance to some dogs in later life — they get caught up with things and often tear, giving the dog a good deal of discomfort.

To remove dew claws is a simple enough operation which most people have done by their veterinary surgeon and some do themselves. The best time to do it is about two to three days after birth, making sure that the dam is out of the way at the time. A pair of sharp, snub-nosed scissors should be sterilized in boiling

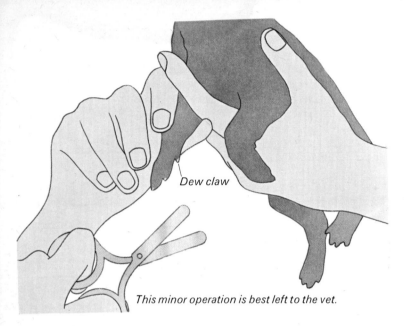

Dew claw

This minor operation is best left to the vet.

water. Great care should be taken with the operation and it is easier done if you have an assistant to hold the puppy for you. The claw or nail is easily located and should be removed with a quick, single snip. The wounds should be dressed at once with substances such as Friars Balsam or crystals of permanganate of potash, which if pressed into the cuts will stem the bleeding instantly. Later, of course, the dam herself will keep the wounds clean with her licking.

Remember to inspect every puppy at least once daily to ensure that all goes well with them and that the operation is successful.

Immunisation

Veterinary science offers the modern dog considerable protection from the virus diseases which might attack it. No one should buy a dog unless he is prepared to have it immunised against these unpleasant diseases, which include Distemper, its off-shoot, Hard Pad, Canine Virus Hepatitis 'known also as Rubarth's Disease) and Leptospiral Jaundice, the last-named arising from contact with the urine of contaminated rats. Leptospiral *canicola* is a less virulent type of bacteria which attacks the dog's kidneys and may contribute to nephritis when the dog is older.

It is an easy matter to have a dog immunised against these scourges. In fact, the first three diseases mentioned above can usually be dealt with by one shot of a special vaccine. This creates a long-term immunity providing it is supplemented with 'booster' doses given annually. When this is done, maximum protection is assured. Immunisation against Leptospirosis is very important as this is a fast-acting killing disease. It can be given at the same time as the other puppy shots but in the case of this malady an added precaution is essential: the place should be thoroughly scoured of rats and the entire area disinfected.

It should be noted that vaccines vary in that long-lasting immunity comes from a live virus source which is really a laboratory dilution of the disease itself. This requires a 'booster' dose every year for maximum effect. Some vaccines are manufactured from a dead virus; their effect is much shorter, usually of just a few months duration.

Teething

A puppy passes through this sometimes painful process between three and six months of age, sometimes earlier in certain breeds. It shows that the permanent or 'second' teeth are coming through. A youngster's appetite is often impaired, either due to debilitation caused by his teething or by the soreness of his gums which restricts eating. Sometimes it is possible to aid the shedding of his milk teeth by taking very loose ones between finger and thumb, pushing them to one side, and easing them gently away, thereby making room for the permanent teeth which will usually be visible. To give the puppy a large marrow or knuckle bone to gnaw on is often effective: this will assist disposal of the unwanted puppy teeth and hasten the advance of the new, permanent set.

There are six incisors both in upper and lower jaws, behind which lie two canines, four premolars, and two molars in the upper jaw – in the lower jaw there are three molars. A puppy is born with permanent molars in the rear of his mouth. The premolars are changed during teething over a six month period and replaced by permanent premolars. The fourth premolar or carnassial tooth is the largest cheek tooth in the upper jaw. The corresponding tooth in the lower jaw is the first large molar. This remains throughout the dog's life. The canine teeth are the largest, the part embedded in the gum being two and a half times as long as the visible part. In effect, there are twenty-two teeth in the lower jaw and twenty

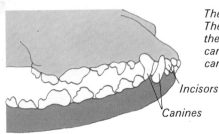

The correct 'scissor bite'.
The upper incisors fit closely over
the lower incisors and the upper
canines fit behind the lower
canines.

Incisors

Canines

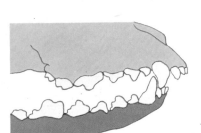

'Overshot'.
The top jaw protrudes over the
lower, causing a space. The
canines are in reverse positions.

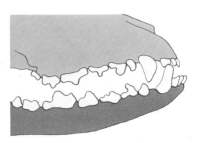

'Undershot'.
The lower incisors protrude beyond
the upper jaw, causing a space
between the upper and lower
canines.

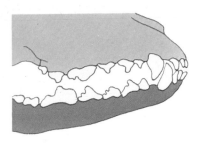

'Pincer' or 'Level bite'.
Teeth of the upper jaw meet the
teeth of the lower jaw.

in the upper jaw, making a usual complement of forty-two in the average dog.

Titbits

Too often pet dogs are allowed to get fat and unhealthy because they are allowed titbits between meals. Many dogs are given sweets and chocolates, fancy biscuits, and indigestible forms of fruit; these do them no good. Too many are allowed to finish up scraps left by the family: residues of meals such as curry, kippers, or smoked cheeses are no good for dogs. Such foods upset their digestion, make them fat, and often useless in the home, and shorten their lives. A dog needs good plain well-balanced food, part meat, part roughage. This should be fed once a day — preferably in the evening with fresh, cool water available all the time. Snacks are not for dogs and the dog owner should learn to disregard the appealing looks directed at him by the dog.

Feeding and exercise

Weaning

How well you wean your puppies will decide much as to their future health and appearance. The dam will normally take responsibility for their milk up to, say, the age of one month, but if she has had a big litter to care for, she is likely to need some assistance by the time her family is three weeks old. This assumes that the bitch's milk has been adequate in volume and of good quality. It will soon become apparent from her puppies' coats and condition if either of these factors is at fault, and you will then have to start weaning very early. However, bitch's milk is essential to the brood while they can get it and no other milk compares with it — as far as puppies are concerned, of course. In *The Complete Dog Breeder's Manual* (1954) by Clifford Hubbard, the author gives an interesting table that reveals the differences between the milk of a bitch and that of four other familiar animals. The table is as follows:

Analyses of milk					
Animal	Sugar	Casein, etc.	Fats	Salts	Water
Dog	*3.1*	*8.0*	*12.0*	*1.2*	*75.5*
Goat	*4.75*	*4.0*	*6.25*	*1.0*	*84.0*
Cat	*5.2*	*7.9*	*3.65*	*0.9*	*82.35*
Cow	*4.85*	*3.75*	*3.7*	*0.6*	*87.1*
Sheep	*4.95*	*4.7*	*5.2*	*0.7*	*84.45*

'Lactol' is an excellent stand-by and can be prepared as a substitute for bitch's milk. Instructions will be found with the preparation. The milk is normally fed at blood heat and, as with hand-rearing, the mixture should be stood in a cup which is in turn stood in a bowl of hot water: this will ensure that the last puppy in the litter is fed with milk of the same temperature as that received by the first youngster. It is not difficult to get a small puppy to lap, just smear a little of the preparation under his lips and wait for it to be taken in. At first progress will be slow, but once the youngster gets the taste he will follow on with enthusiasm. Every puppy has to be fed individually at first and once you have them all lapping with confidence they can be introduced to a communal dish. By this time the dam's burden of feeding has been eased a little, and although they will still be at her teats, at least they will not be dragging at her excessively. Before putting down the communal dish, make sure they have not been near their dam for an hour or more previously. The average puppy can be left to get on with his meal without hogging from his fellows, but it is advisable to watch them all the time when feeding. Try to keep the feeding trough at a raised level, i.e. a little off the ground. This will ensure that the puppies do not fall into the food, and it will aid towards a better posture and improve the youngster's general bearing.

Feeding can be stepped up from the 'Lactol' routine after three or four days. The extra diet can include minced boiled tripe, poached egg and very lightly boiled milk puddings, and finely shredded or minced raw fresh meat. The meat should be introduced in easy stages, but the quantity should be increased gradually until it represents about 50 per cent of the intake. Care should be taken that not too much is put down at a time. To avoid distension and also digestive discomforts, it is best to divide a normal daily intake into four 'sittings', spread over a twelve hour period. By the time the puppies are six weeks old they will have grown quite a bit and will be increasing their weight weekly. About this time, or even earlier, the dam herself will be disgorging some of her food for her puppies' benefit. This a natural action and need not perturb a breeder who has not witnessed it before, but its advantages are mixed. The puppies will rush at the partly-digested food and gobble it up, so you should make sure that the meals you give the dam at this time do not contain either food that is too rich for puppies or food cut up too large to suit their digestive system. Also, if the dam is allowed to disgorge food too often she is going to fall badly out of condition and this is no time for that to happen. In fact, she must now be built up well with high-protein food with plenty of fresh raw meat, although fluids can be cut down severely as her milk supply must be minimal.

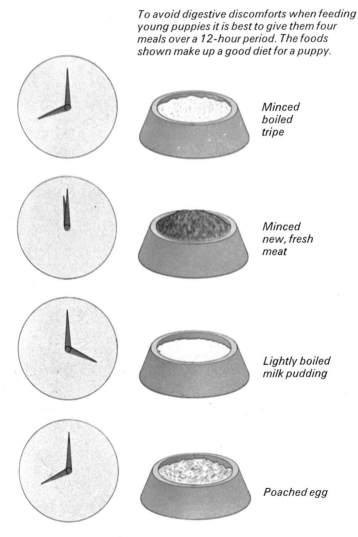

To avoid digestive discomforts when feeding young puppies it is best to give them four meals over a 12-hour period. The foods shown make up a good diet for a puppy.

Minced boiled tripe

Minced new, fresh meat

Lightly boiled milk pudding

Poached egg

The puppies themselves should be drinking plenty of milk, as milk is essential for good growth and bone. At six weeks of age they will be on four meals a day, two meat meals and two milky feeds, given to them alternately. They should by now be quite independent of their dam's milk supply. The amount of food will need stepping-up: the amount – also the quality – will determine their development in the next few months. Do not overfeed them: it is important to watch the litter at feeding time so that you can gain an intimate knowledge of each puppy's requirements. In the next week you can reduce the actual number of meals to three, but this does not mean the quantity has to be reduced, quite the opposite, in fact.

During the whole of the puppy-rearing term, from weaning to independence, it is important to inspect every youngster after its meal. The nose and mouth will need wiping over to remove waste-food encrustment, and the under-tail area and the genitals should be examined after motions have been passed; they should be cleaned-up if necessary.

Worming

As this is a matter which requires attention during the weaning period it can be included in this section. The most commonly encountered worm in puppies is the roundworm. This is a parasite rather like vermicelli and is creamy-white in colour: all puppies are thought to be infested to a greater or lesser degree. The dam herself probably passes them on to her embryonic young but they are easily enough acquired by puppies from the faeces of infected dogs, or from eggs taken from their dam's teats in course of feeding.

The infested puppy seldom thrives until the pest has been eradicated. The youngster's appetite usually falls off, although instances have been noted when a puppy has become ravenous. The coat begins to 'stare' and divide, while motions seem 'jellied' or very loose, indicating an upset stomach. There are many good proprietary vermifuges and vermicides on the market today, and the average experienced breeder/owner prefers to use one of these quite early in the youngster's life. At one time it was not considered prudent to worm a puppy before it was at least five weeks old, but veterinary medicine now permits earlier dosing with no ill-effects. For those who do not fancy the task of worming, the veterinary surgeon will attend to the matter for a nominal fee. When expelled (if a vermifuge is used), the worms will appear in a tightly-knit skein and will probably surprise you by their number.

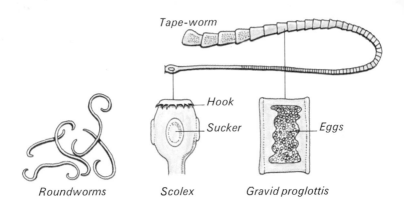

Tape-worm

Hook

Sucker

Eggs

Roundworms　　Scolex　　Gravid proglottis

Burn them at once and disinfect the area of operations, at the same time cleaning up the now relieved puppy in his anal region.

The tapeworm is rather different. It attaches itself by a sort of hook to the intestinal wall and is made up with a number of segments: small at the head end, but gradually increasing in size towards the 'tail' or opposite end. Each segment is really a worm in its own right and on breaking away from the main stem and being passed through its host it may become ingested by an animal such as the sheep, horse, rabbit, or fox. A flea can pass on the worm to the dog, who can also acquire the parasite from the viscera of an infected produce animal or from rabbit caught in the wild.

This worm is less frequently met with than the roundworm, but its effect is rather less pleasant. It can be noted, as a rule, when the grain-like segments, which comprise the main shaft of the worm, are seen adhering to the dog's anus or are evident in his motions. It is best to ask your vet to deal with this worm as he is much more likely to do this effectively than you would with a home remedy. Once expelled, the dog's condition will improve noticeably within a few days, his coat will become glossy and healthy and the strong body odour, usually so evident in dogs with tapeworm, will disappear.

Note that every puppy, before being sold, should be wormed (for roundworm) and this should be done at least three days before he goes to his new home. The breeder should make sure that the worming has not adversely affected the youngster's stomach and that his motions are firm and healthy by the time he reaches his new owner.

Adult feeding

One is inclined perhaps to consider what the dog would eat were he in the wild state. This may be a useful guide but the findings should not be followed slavishly.

It is important that he has fresh raw meat as his main and staple diet. By all means get him used to eating cooked meat, canned proprietary dog foods, carefully boned steamed white fish and so on. But do this only if you cannot lay your hands on the fresh raw meat. Many dogs, having been fed only meat, will refuse other food and such a dog can prove a worry to his owner if meat is not available. A dog prefers his meat in large lumps so he can tear off the pieces he wants to eat and enjoy it at will, Few dog owners feed their dogs in this way, preferring to cut up the meat into manageable chunks. The meat should be butcher's meat, shin of beef being particularly beneficial, and at a price to suit most pockets. Many breeders complain at the cost of butcher's meat, which is certainly high and it seems sensible if you cannot afford to keep a dog on such foods, to try to adapt him to meals which will probably cost less yet provide for him just as well. There are so many processed and prepared dog foods on the market today, most of them offered by highly reputable firms with up-to-date laboratories and factories, that one cannot lightly reject them when planning a dog's menu at an economic price. Some people think highly of offal, paunches, and such things. These are good, but like liver give best results when fed about once a week rather than daily. Dog biscuits are essential, there being many different kinds to choose from, and you will soon get to know what your dog likes best and what suits him. Following any trial of biscuits and/or new type of feeding, always keep an eye on the dog's main motion that day and the following days. This will tell you if the experimental stuff suits his stomach or not. Fish is excellent food for the dog, and the fishmonger has quite a large variety of cheap fish suited to him. Fish feeding should be included in the menu no more than twice a week at the most. It should be used, like some of the canned foods, more as a change of diet or to add zest to an ordinary dish rather than as a staple diet. Make sure with fish that every bone has been removed; it is best served boiled or steamed, from which methods the dog gains most nutriment. Eggs and milk are of course essentials, especially milk, and can be presented in a number of attractive ways. Certainly a dog ought to have available a bowl of fresh milk daily. Most vegetables and potatoes are not particularly suitable for dogs and if forced upon them usually cause digestive upsets. The dog himself knows this instinctively and confines himself as a rule to green grass, usually eaten as an emetic.

The average adult dog can exist well on a single sound meal a day. But a certain standard of condition and muscle has to be maintained and to this end the breeder must strive. Obviously, if your dog looks scrawny and thin it is reasonable to assume he is not getting enough meat and the amount must be increased accordingly. If a dog appears hungry it is apparent that he can be fed more, but always keep an eye on your dog when he is feeding. You will see how he tackles his meal; if he goes through it fast and seems to seek more, then it is probable he could do with more, but if he gets two thirds of the way through the meal and then eats the rest as though he could not care, he probably does not care for more and your quantity is slightly in excess of enough.

All dog feeding and care is largely a matter of common sense and you should learn to know your dog so well that you will become aware of any variation, however slight, in his manner and/ or make-up. Additives, such as commercially marketed yeast extracts, are extremely useful in creating a healthy appetite and aiding the dog's mental outlook. Most breeders keep a stock of

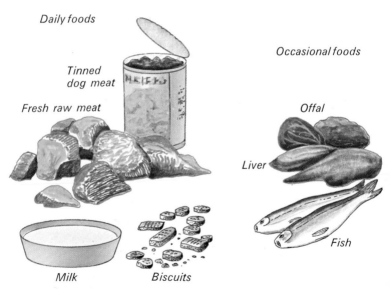

Daily foods

Tinned dog meat

Fresh raw meat

Occasional foods

Offal

Liver

Fish

Milk

Biscuits

these useful tablets by them and have found them extremely beneficial. Cod-liver oil is useful in the winter months, with olive oil better, perhaps, when the weather is hot. Malt extract is recommended as a body-builder. It is not necessary to give more than one teaspoonful of these oils daily to an adult. Cod-liver oil is available, and is also cheaper, in veterinary form. Vitamins too can be obtained in capsules and tablets, and these can be used with advantage, although it is advisable to have the doses prescribed by your veterinary surgeon or other professional adviser.

Never feed poultry and game unless just the carved plain flesh is given. The bones are very dangerous to a dog. If your dog catches a rabbit and eats it the same day he will seldom come to any harm, but if the carcass remains to be eaten a day or so later, the bones will have brittled and can then constitute a real danger to him.

Many breeders are inclined to worry about the growth and development of their puppies, wondering if the youngsters are progressing as well as can be expected. Individuals vary considerably, much depending on the size of the litter, health of the dam, and the manner in which post-natal care and feeding has been managed.

Exercise
This is a subject to worry some owners as many are never quite sure whether they give enough time to exercising their dogs. It is reasonable to say, with some reservations, that the larger the dog the more exercise he will require. It should be borne in mind that some fast-growing big dogs at around six months of age have outgrown their strength and a lot of heavy field work would do them nothing but harm. The wise owner of an Old English Sheepdog or an Irish Wolfhound would take it very easy at exercising his dog until it was nearly a year old. From that age, of course, these breeds and other similar big breeds can take plenty of exercise. Conversely, some small dogs, especially those in the Terrier class, can walk for miles without showing signs of tiredness, and yet such dogs and Toys can adapt themselves to minimal exercise, unlike the larger varieties and Hounds.

It is only fair to give your dog regular and sufficient exercise. No one should keep a dog unless he is prepared to sacrifice at least some of his time to this end. By exercising a dog you keep him fit and well-conditioned and his nails short. Regular walking should be on the leash, for he will gain more benefit from steady pace walking on hard ground than he will from dashing about on

Utility Dogs

Chow-Chow

Miniature Poodle

Shih Tzu

grassland. Nevertheless, dogs love the latter sport, especially if there is some ball-throwing involved and this should at times be incorporated in his exercise. To work out how much exercise a dog needs, his owner must consider the dog's environment. A dog who has free access to a yard or garden may well need less exercise than an animal whose hours are largely spent confined to an upstairs flat. Then again, the specific breed of dog should be a guide – a Beagle will need more open ground work than say a Boston Terrier living in a penthouse apartment. In any case a dog should be exercised *at least* once daily. How far you take him on his walks should be a matter decided by observation and experience. If he seems tired turn around and take him home. A young growing dog cannot take too much walking, neither can a dog who is off-colour, and many of the light-boned breeds, and Toys especially, will weary quickly if taken too far. When out, keep an eye on the dog's motions and his manner of passing them. A lot can be learned of his state of health in this way. Motions should be firm, well moulded, and not looser than say the consistency of porridge. Diarrhoea points to an upset stomach and should be dealt with at once. Constipation and light-coloured motions suggest too much biscuit meal and not enough meat, indicating the need for a better-balanced diet. A dog who 'toboggans' his hind quarters along the ground may be suffering from worms or clogged anal glands and this will require his owner's or a veterinary surgeon's attention. The anal glands are set just at the entrance of the anus, one on either side. Originally, when the dog was wild they held a pungent fluid which could be ejected at will to fix a tracking scent. With the domesticity of the dog the glands have fallen into virtual disuse and may become stopped up with waste matter, causing the dog distress and discomfort. The offending matter is usually dispelled by lifting the dog's tail, placing a pad of cotton wool over the anal region and squeezing it out.

The best time for exercising is morning and evening, perhaps a minimum of twenty minutes on both occasions. Both periods should be with the dog on his leash, but occasionally the exercise should be given with the animal loose in some safe park, well away from traffic, farm stock, and other perils and temptations. The keynote of successful exercising is *regularity*. Try to keep to specific times when exercising. The dog will become attuned to the hour when he goes out and his natural functions will adapt themselves to these times, keeping him fit and healthy. Guard against the bad-weather months when you may be sorely tempted to hug the fire rather than turn out into the cold and wet with your dog.

Vitamins

Protein is the most important factor in a dog's diet. But if the best results are to be achieved, vitamins and minerals must be introduced in correct balance, and so should adequate carbohydrates and fats. Protein makes for body growth, fat gives energy, as do carbohydrates. Minerals such as calcium and phosphorus are needed for teeth and bone, and aid the heart and blood system. Iron, copper, and cobalt contribute to healthy blood.

Essential vitamins to a dog's health exist in natural feeding and come from sunshine. Because it is not always easy to provide these naturally, the dog owner should study the worth of vitamins to be found in home produce and feeding.

VITAMIN A. This is found in fish, liver, oils, heart, eggs, and milk. It is useful in building up body resistance to infection and contributes to strong bone in puppies. It is believed to be helpful in countering weaknesses of the eye. Raw parsley and carrots are strong in this vitamin.

VITAMIN B. This vitamin is found in a variety of foods. It exists in milk, meat, eggs, yeast, and wheat germ. Liver is a well-known source. It is beneficial to the nervous system and to skin and coat. Teething puppies benefit from its application.

VITAMIN C. This is the well-known 'sunshine' vitamin. It is available to the dog through grass, and is essential for growth, good teeth, and a good skin. Milk also contains this vitamin.

VITAMIN D. This is present in fish oils, butter, liver, and the yolk of egg. It is another 'sunshine' vitamin.

VITAMIN E. Found mainly in germ oil, it has a distinct effect on fertility in both dog and bitch. In the former it will bolster his potency and in the female this vitamin will work against foetal disorders and abnormalities.

As a rough guide to feeding, adult dogs require about $\frac{1}{3}$ oz. meat for each 1 lb. bodyweight daily. Very young, growing dogs may require rather more than this, say $\frac{1}{2}$ oz. per lb. bodyweight. To meat rations should be added a certain amount of roughage in the form of biscuit meal, dog biscuit, cereal, etc. This makes for energy, especially in a working dog. Overweight dogs are usually thus because they have been given more energising food than they need and not enough exercise to burn off the excess fat. As with all things, moderation in feeding and dosage is important to good health and proper functioning. Meals and medicines and vitamins need to be supplied with care and in careful balance. If in doubt on the subject speak to your veterinarian.

Daily meat requirements for your dog.

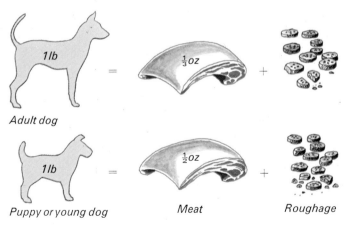

Adult dog

$\frac{1}{3}$oz

Puppy or young dog

$\frac{1}{2}$oz

Meat

Roughage

General training

Early discipline

No one enjoys having an ill-trained dog and it is often patently clear that the dog himself does not enjoy being ill-trained! He does not want to be continually reprimanded and shouted at, which so many owners seem to do merely because they have not bothered to show their dog what to do and how to do it. A badly trained dog reflects on his owner's ability as a trainer.

Many of the pedigree breeds have strong and positive characters, some are powerful and require particularly firm handling, others are perhaps temperamental, even shy, and require a certain amount of 'understanding' and special care in the way they are trained. Whatever the type of dog, kind yet firm handling is essential in order to maintain the animal comfortably within the family circle and train him to do what *you* want him to do rather than have him do what he wants to do.

Most people prefer a puppy to train. It is usually easier to do this than to work with a dog of over six months who may well have started his life in a poor environment and has come to you completely untrained. A small puppy straight from the nest soon gets to know his way around and to know what you expect of him. Be firm with him right from the start. Too many owners laugh and enjoy a youngster's antics and mischievous behaviour, its exuberance and clumsiness – only to realise when it is rather too late that the dog has grown up with the bad habits. It may then be difficult to break him of these unwanted characteristics; certainly it will need a good deal of hard work and patience on the part of the owner to do so. This emphasises the need for firmness in training right from the start.

All animals, even fish, are strict enforcers of their territorial rights. Show your puppy where he is to sleep, where he can roam, and the areas of the home which are forbidden to him, as soon as you get him home, and guide him constantly in strict observance of these 'home rules'. You will soon cultivate a pleasant companion.

Decide on a name for your new puppy as soon as possible. A dog needs a name to facilitate his training in or around the home and a name that lends itself easily to a note of command, i.e. of one or no more than two syllables. It is advisable to select a name that is in accord with the breed or general appearance of the dog. A name like 'Thor' while ideal for your Boxer or Bulldog would appear incongruous if applied to one of the Toy breeds.

Once a name has been chosen use it at every opportunity, even make opportunities of calling or directing the puppy with the use of his name. He will learn speedily and seem to cherish the sound of his personal name.

If, unfortunately, the dog has to change hands, the new owner should try to keep to the name or at least select a name that closely resembles the original one.

One of the first words a puppy must learn is 'No!' With this word freely and sharply used he will quickly learn the difference between good and bad habits. All puppies are inclined to destructiveness, some much more than others. Terriers are apt to chew more than the Bull Breeds, although a gnawing Bulldog can create much more damage if left to his own devices. It must be remembered that a young puppy with teething pains needs to relieve them, and what could be better than a nice table leg? Of course, the best way to preserve the table leg, the carpet, and your carpet slippers is to ensure that the puppy is not left alone for too long. Even when semi-trained, a puppy is inclined to slip back into bad habits and if a virile youngster with sharp teeth is left unheeded in the dining room and he chews up everything in

1 Stop a puppy from chewing by pulling him away with the word 'NO'.

2 If he continues, pull him away sharply with the same command in a scolding voice.

3 If he returns, repeat and offer a marrow bone.

sight, then it is more likely to be his owner's fault than his. If he starts to chew some object, pull him away from it with the word 'No!'. He will look at you in some surprise and possibly make a move back to the scene to start again. This time, pull him away more sharply with the same command in a loud scolding tone. If you have a nice, safe marrow bone handy, give him that and encourage him to chew on it. If he starts to do this, then praise him with the words *Good Dog!*. The tone of the two different commands will soon register with the average puppy and he will know when he is doing right and pleasing you and when his actions annoy you. Be kind yet strict in your commands. With puppies of some physical substance, a firm tap with the word 'No' will not come amiss, but such admonishment should be light: puppies get frightened easily and can quickly lose confidence in the teacher.

Training to the lead
The owner who will get best results in training his dog is the one with patience. Considerable patience is required, especially with some breeds where obstinacy is a distinct characteristic in their make-up. The Bulldog, for example, although a loyal and amiable dog likes to have his own way at times and may not respond to training quite as speedily as the Alsatian or Sheepdog. The former is a breed indoctrinated with disciplinary training, the latter with a natural tendency to obey command. An owner should associate himself with the disposition of his dog and work on his charge in such a way that the dog will not be ruffled or upset during the course of his training. The voice should always be firm, but calm; the touch gentle, but positive. The trainer should never lose his temper, although at times he may be tempted to do so. A young dog especially, reacts badly to an angry shout and rough treatment, and an especially sensitive animal may well be ruined early in his career with such ill-considered handling.

The puppy should be got used to a collar early in his life. At first he will fidget and scratch at the unwanted piece of leather around his neck, but within an hour or so he will accept it. Care should be taken with some of the longer-coated breeds that a collar is not allowed to remain round the neck while the animal is asleep: its pressure and movement could ruff up and derange the hair. It is best to start with a thin, lightweight collar – the strap form is probably best and cheapest at this stage. Make sure it is not fixed too tightly – on the other hand the dog should not be able to back

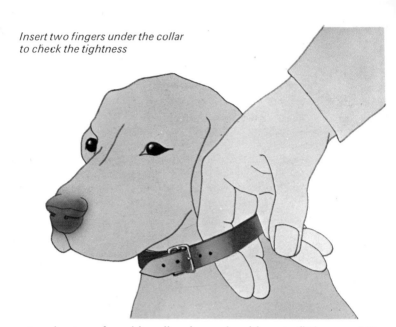

Insert two fingers under the collar to check the tightness

out and escape from his collar. A *rough* guide as to fitting would be that two fingers should be placed between the collar and the dog's neck before fastening the buckle. Dogs grow quickly and collar fitting should be inspected regularly — at least two or three times a week, especially with the bigger and heavier varieties. Once the puppy has accepted his collar you can fix a lead to it and give him some exercise up and down the garden path. He may wriggle like an eel at first and pull and drag on the lead, but after a short while he will begin to understand what you want of him. If he sits down and refuses to move, do not pull him — go behind him, pat him and stroke him, and with a gentle push you will soon start him again on a forward movement. Guide him alongside you, always on the left side as this is the approved and conventional positional method of training; it is also one of the first exercises the dog should know. It is known as 'heeling'.

With the dog placed always on the left side of the trainer, the lead should rest in the trainer's right hand, loosely held so that it is slack and it loops half-way between the dog's collar and the ground. The pupil's right shoulder (in the case of a medium-sized breed) should be level with the trainer's knee. The dog must be encouraged to walk freely and with confidence. He may thrust too far ahead in which case the trainer should pull back sharply on the lead with the command 'Heel', getting the dog back into line with his knee. Be sure that the dog is suitably rewarded with some form of titbit. He will soon catch on and realise that if he does well and obeys the command he will get something out of it. Remember to keep to the one word 'Heel'. The dog will get to know what it means and may be persuaded to keep from moving too far ahead if the trainer keeps some small titbit concealed in his left hand which is then held in line with his left leg. Should the pupil surge ahead, the command 'Heel' will soon bring him back so that in due course, if and when the leash is detached from the collar, he will need no command, no correction, but walk loose in what is known as 'heel free' manner alongside his owner-handler.

Words of command

'Sit' and 'Down' are two important commands, especially for the dog who is to live in the family circle. At this stage it is worth mentioning that a dog can be trained by a very quick method of commanding him to do what he does naturally! This may be better explained by saying that when your puppy is about to sit down of his own accord you command 'Sit' and as soon as you see him begin to flop out or lie down you command 'Down'. He will soon get the idea and when you settle down to serious training in these two words, your work will already be half done.

The best way to get the dog to sit is to walk with him in the heel position, your right hand holding the leash, your left hand ready down the line of your leg. Stop and command 'Sit', lifting the leash with your right hand to raise the puppy's head while at the same time pressing down on to his haunches with your left hand until he sits. Remain stationary while conducting this exercise, for if you move forward or backward the dog will be thrown off balance and lose the benefit of the intended action. Should he go down too far and assume a lying position, it will probably mean that you have let the leash in your right hand slide down too far. Never jerk up with the leash in such an instance, but draw it up firmly with your left hand pressing down on his haunches, still repeating the command 'Sit'. The entire exercise should be carried through calmly and firmly, even for a few seconds longer than might seem necessary. In this way the dog will learn what you want. To achieve the 'Down' position one merely goes a stage further than the '*Sit*', easing his front legs gently away and from under his body, commanding 'Down' at the same time. Many trainers prefer to get a dog first into the sit position and follow up immediately with the 'Down' command. Remember that to complete both exercises properly the dog should sit or lie down with his head immediately facing front, his body set squarely. If he places himself diagonally, nudge his quarters to the right or left so that he is placed directly forward.

Dogs generally find it difficult to stay in one position for any length of time, especially if unattended. The down position being the most comfortable train him from there to 'Stay'. As you give the command, step back a pace or two. If he fidgets and gets up, command him back to the 'Down' position, repeating at once the command 'Stay'. He will soon learn what you want until eventually you can move a good distance from him without him rising. Eventually you will be able to go completely out of his sight and remain thus for fairly long periods. However, a dog might not know where you have gone and worry about it, so the exercise should not be conducted indiscriminately, or for too long, especially with a young puppy.

A dog who will not come when called is a nuisance, not only to his owner but often to himself. Never chase him but try to

Lead held in right hand, dog on left

'Heel'. Pull back on lead, try to keep the dog's shoulders level with your legs.

'Sit'. Keep the dog's head raised with the lead, press down on dog's hindquarters.

'Down'. From the sitting position, gently lift the dog's front legs away from under him.

coax him to you with a titbit, all the time saying 'Come'. When he does come give him the titbit, a pat on the head, and a few words of praise. He will soon learn that something pleasant happens at the end of the command 'Come'. Unless absolutely necessary, do not put him on the leash immediately you have secured him. He will associate the 'Come' exercise with the end of his freedom and may not prove very obliging on future occasions. You may find with young puppies that they respond better to you if you adopt a kneeling position when you call them to you. Never punish or otherwise distress a dog when you have retrieved him or you will never get him to obey the command 'Come'. A difficult pupil may require training with a light check cord attached to his collar. This should not be used to drag him back to you, but rather to monitor his movements and to ease him back. The voice and the titbit should play the main parts in this particular training exercise.

Although it is perfectly natural for a dog to sniff at every corner and lamp-post, it is a most unhygienic habit and is probably the cause of much canine ill-health. It is advisable to train your dog to ignore such 'attractions' with the simple command 'Leave'. The word should be accompanied by a sharp jerk on the leash until he will obey just on the word alone. The same exercise and command can be used at any time if you wish your dog to ignore any object in the street or home.

Pulling is a habit which needs correction from the outset. Many dogs once they are leashed start to pull and scramble forward, dragging their owners behind them. Not only is it irritating, but the scrambling-forward action of the animal, if persisted with, is liable to throw out the shoulders and spoil his action for life. This is especially important if you have a dog you plan to exhibit, for good deportment is essential in the show ring.

Keep the pupil on a short leash held in the left hand. Carry a rolled-up newspaper in the right hand. Every time the dog pulls forward give the command 'Heel' and thrust the end of the newspaper in front of his nose to make him falter, at the same time easing him back in his tracks. Alternatively, the newspaper can be slapped against your right leg. He will not like the noise it makes and this will cause him to respond more sharply to the command. On a larger animal, if the roll has to be used on him for correction it will not hurt him, but the noise of impact should deter and curb him. Some trainers use choke or slip chains, but such are for medium- to large-sized breeds and should never be used with puppies of any breed or with Toy dogs. In any case, a choke chain needs to be put on properly; incorrectly fixed it is cruel and can cause damage. If you buy one make sure its method of application is properly explained to you.

Jumping up is a disconcerting habit that can make both the dog and his owner unpopular. Clean clothes and hosiery are short-lived when an exuberant dog bounds at your visitors, even strangers in the street, and the habit is one to correct immediately. Apart from such drastic remedies as treading on a persistent offender's back toes or pointing your bent knee against him as he jumps, thereby throwing him backwards, corrective action should always be accompanied with the sharp command 'No'. A firm push away will often do the trick, but this is clearly a matter requiring rigid action on an owner's part. It has been found that bending down to a 'jumper', will curb his leap, but neither visitors nor strangers are likely to cooperate satisfactorily in this respect so it is advisable to break the dog of this annoying habit before it becomes fixed.

Road sense
The dog should always be on the leash when walking out. Get him used to the 'Sit' exercise for a few moments before you cross the road. Stand with him while he sits there, then when the road is clear say 'Over' and start off for the other side of the road. Always try to use the authorised pedestrian crossing as the dog will get used to these too. When waiting at the kerb to cross, try to let him see *why* you are waiting and *why* you cross at a given time.

When he wants to do his business, draw him gently over to the gutter and encourage him to do it there. Most local authorities impose penalties on owners who allow their dogs to foul the pavements and the same should apply to other public places. If you can catch your dog just when he is about to squat you should always try to ease him to some quiet unattended area. Better still, try to get him to relieve himself in a quiet spot before taking him into the town centre.

Maintenance and care

Grooming

The wise owner will ensure that his dog, whether just a home pet or a pedigree show dog, is groomed and given a health inspection daily. Once these exercises have become established as a daily practice, the time involved in doing them gets less and the grooming period itself minimal. Brushing makes a dog tidy and the action of the brush stimulates the skin and body muscles, bringing on a sense of well-being and self-respect. This is particularly important in a dog that is intended for show-ring work.

Getting a puppy to stand and show some interest in his grooming is important. It is particularly important to get a long-haired dog used to grooming, especially if he is a show dog : such a dog should be taught to lie passively on its sides and extend all four legs. Small breeds, of course, can be groomed satisfactorily from an owner's lap, although generally speaking it is best to get a dog used to a table top set at the right height for working comfort.

Coats vary as do breeds. Good coats are usually inherited from the ancestral line and with a dog whose coat is *naturally* poor, there is little to be done. However, good coats are also dependent on a dog's good health, ample exercise, and a well-balanced diet in which fat plays an important part. His food intake should include roughly a quarter of fat in cold winter months, rather less during the summer. This can be made up with linseed oil and suet additives or malt extract, but olive oil may prove better in the summer season.

This book is not able to encompass the grooming requirements of the many different breeds that exist today. Therefore, the choice of equipment is better decided on the advice to be received from your local pet-store specialist or breeder. Generally speaking, it is best to purchase a good hound-glove, a soft chamois polisher, and a comb that suits your dog's coat. Buy the best you can afford : brass combs with steel pins coated with chromium serve well as they do not bend and can be boiled or washed in disinfectant. Make sure the teeth ends are blunt and will not scratch the dog : in any case, dog combs should be held and used in a slanting position to avoid doing this. You will also want a good brush, and here the choice is wide and individual preference, which comes with practice, will guide you in due course. For your initial purchase it is best to refer to the breeder from whom you bought your pedigree puppy. For example, a Labrador requires firm and vigorous brushing, whereas a Brussels Griffon needs more careful treatment; for the first you would buy a strong bristle brush and for the latter a soft bristle brush such as a small baby's brush. Providing you remember that small breeds require soft brushing and the medium to large breeds can take stronger handling you will not go far wrong, but bear in mind that the length of bristle on the brush should be such that it will penetrate from the surface of the coat to the dog's skin. Should your dog be a cross-bred or mongrel, the best way is to work to the same formula as this when you buy your equipment.

Smooth-coated dogs, such as Smooth Fox Terriers, are easy to groom. With such coats, brushing should always be in the direction in which the hair grows, going firmly over the head, neck, back, and body, brushing out all dust and dandruff. Then brush the hind parts, all four legs, and the dog's front. The work can be finished with the use of a hound-glove and then a polish with a silk or nylon cloth. Some owners use a proprietary spray to produce a sparkle on the coat, but this is a matter for individual preference. Most pet stores stock these sprays. and/or lotions. Hand massage over the dog's body before completion will do much to tone him up and keep the skin supple.

Long-coated breeds take more time and are rather more difficult to groom, but speed and aptitude come with practice. Generally speaking, a coarse open-toothed comb is best for these breeds, as matting and tangles are likely to be encountered and the owner must avoid hurting his dog during grooming or it will become shy of being brushed. Tangles must be teased out and the offending tuft should be taken between finger and thumb of one hand and supported close to the dog's body while the other hand gets to work with the comb. Any pulling that has to be done should be between the two hands, never from the body. Occasionally, an owner may have to soak a tangle or mat in almond oil to release the knotted coat.

The best way to groom the long-haired varieties is to do the coat in sections, commencing at the stomach and working up to the underjaw. With the dog lying on its side, lift up a layer of coat at a time then brush it downwards with firm even movements. Make sure that every part of the coat is brushed to its full length and depth with the brush going right down to the skin. If the dog is very long-haired over the head and eyes you may have to plait or secure the hair back to allow access to the dog's face.

The grooming requirements of different breeds of dog vary, but generally it is best to purchase a chamois polisher, and a brush or comb that suits your dog's coat.

Smooth-coated dogs are easy to groom; brush in the direction that the hair lies.

Long-coated dogs take more time and are not so easy to groom. The best way is to do the coat in sections with the dog on its side.

Some breeds need certain methods of brushing in order to encourage growth and positioning of the coat in the 'right' places. This is done in the main for exhibition work and need not concern the average dog owner. Owners of breeds such as Pomeranians and Chow Chows – usually know what to do with their dogs, and there are handbooks and standard works on most breeds.

Extra attention has to be paid to ear fringes, mane, and the various featherings that are inevitably found on most long-coated dogs and which have varying degrees of importance to the specialist breeder. These features need careful combing and brushing to make the best of their appearance. In between the toes the hair sometimes grows too profusely, it should be snipped out carefully to an acceptable minimum and finished neatly – in the case of certain breeds to the form demanded by their breed Standards. It should be noted that some of the long-coated breeds are probably better not brushed, most of the work on the coat being done with a smooth-toothed steel comb if an undercoat is not wanted. Extra care has to be taken with the silky- and soft-coated breeds as much damage can be done to their coats with rough grooming. Grooming should be right down to the skin and only smooth combs and soft-bristle brushes used. Some breeds, such

Working Dogs

Alsatian (German Shepherd)

Shetland Sheepdog

50

as the previously mentioned Pomeranian, have rather harsh coats on the surface with a dense undercoat which must not be combed except when the individual is moulting. Failure to observe this point will result in the comb removing part of the undercoat that gives a Pomeranian the desired 'stand-off' effect.

A dog usually moults twice a year, once in the spring and again in autumn. This is his natural moult, but sometimes moulting is met with in dogs that are sick and in bitches during the post-natal period. Temperature usually decides when a moulting takes place, the shedding taking place with distinct rises or falls. Some dogs seem to moult consistently throughout the year, thereby causing their owners much annoyance. To alleviate the domestic situation, at least to some extent, such dogs should be brushed several times a day. The friction of the brush will help to stimulate the skin and tone up the muscles, disposing of dead hair and activating the growth of new. Poodles and certain breeds of foreign origin, moult, but in a different manner – the hair instead of shedding on to carpets and furniture adheres to the new coat as it grows through. The best type of brush for Poodles is a nylon hair brush. To remove unwanted hair in the home a vacuum cleaner will suffice but a fold

Toy Dogs

Pekingese

Yorkshire Terrier

Chihuahua

of adhesive tape laid across the region affected will prove as effective as some of the static clothes brushes on the market.

Wire-haired breeds are relatively simple to groom, although if you own a Wire-haired Fox Terrier, for example, the work required to fashion his coat for show-ring acceptance is perhaps a job for the professional trimmer. However, it is a craft that can be learned by the novice, although not at once: the preparatory work on the coat prior to an important show requires about two months of careful attention to the different stages entailed. Experience rather than book learning teaches the fancier to complete a perfect presentation. Only plucking with the finger and thumb is countenanced by the professional, as this is believed to produce the best results. Mechanical aids such as electric and hand clippers are certainly speedier and in the hands of a competent person can show quite good results. There are training courses arranged for novices by some of the big kennels, and for the owner of a Wire-haired Fox Terrier, who wishes to prepare his own dog for show, much can be learned from such establishments.

However, pet dogs can be dealt with at home and are usually trimmed, quite simply, with scissors and/or clippers, the main purpose being to get the dog ready for warmer days when his coat would be an encumbrance, as well as to dispose of dead hair. The golden rule with such dogs is to groom the coat daily: a neglected coat will become thick, woolly, and probably unmanageable. You will need a strong bristle brush capable of getting right down to skin level and a wide-toothed steel comb. Remember that the coat of a Wire-haired Fox Terrier is particularly dense, not unlike coconut matting, which twists and crinkles but does not curl. Below the top coat is a soft, finer protective undercoat. Normally the Wire-haired Fox Terrier's coat is so dense that even when it is parted with the fingers the dog's skin cannot be seen. This is why it is so vital to the well-being of the animal and his coat to remove all dead and unwanted hair and to keep the skin in good and clean condition.

A health check
The daily grooming session is a good time to check over your dog to ensure he is free from minor health disorders capable of affecting skin, feet, and teeth – in fact any part of the body. By so doing the dog can be kept in good order and anything wrong can be detected in its earliest stages and probably corrected without much trouble.

Much can be learned from the bloom, gloss, or texture of a dog's coat. An out-of-condition dog seldom sports a good coat – it becomes dull, ragged, and 'stares' in the case of smooth-coated breeds. This means that it stands off from the body in an untidy manner, indicating the need for some form of conditioning medicine to be prescribed by your veterinary surgeon.

Eyes should be bright and clear and free from any form of discharge. Always wipe over a dog's eyes before you commence grooming. A cotton-wool pad which has been soaked in a mild boric solution (5 ml. boracic crystals in $\frac{1}{2}$ pt. hot water) will be found best for doing this. Ulcers are best dealt with professionally. Extra care has to be taken in the examination of breeds with prominent eyes, dogs such as Pugs, Boston Terriers, and Brussels Griffons being especially prone to eye damage.

A dog's nose should be cool and clean. A warm nose (especially on a dog that has just woken up) is not necessarily an indication of impending sickness, but the nose should never remain dry for any length of time. Mucus from the nostrils may suggest viral infection, although possibly it may be no more than a cold. Always wipe over the nose in such cases with a clean cloth and smear the nostril gently with olive oil.

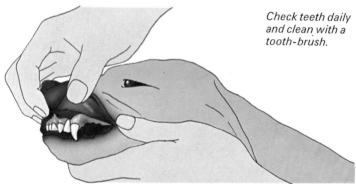

Check teeth daily and clean with a tooth-brush.

Teeth should be brushed daily using an ordinary medium bristle tooth brush in a rotary action. The water used should be warm and have had a small pinch of salt dissolved in it. Some people use a piece of rag instead of a tooth brush, but whichever you use include the gums in the cleaning movement as this will stimulate them. Guard against tartar on the enamel of the teeth ; this takes the form of a hard, brown deposit which if allowed to encrust the enamel will severely limit the life of the teeth. It can be scraped off by any veterinary surgeon, or home scrapers can be purchased in most pet stores. Always inspect a young puppy's teeth daily, especially when he is shedding his first (or milk) teeth. The permanent teeth will be pushing through the gums at from three to four months of age, and whereas the milk teeth should fall out as the permanent teeth come through, it sometimes happens that a few are retained. When this happens, the milk tooth should be gently eased out without hurting the puppy, otherwise the on-coming permanent tooth may be pushed out of place and cause the adult to have a faulty mouth. These first teeth are often very soft and break easily so take care if you have to extract one manually. A broken tooth may leave some fragments in the gum and cause an abscess. A puppy has usually completed dentition by the time it is six months old. Teething is materially assisted by giving the youngster dry biscuits or 'safe' hard bones to gnaw.

The feet should be inspected in between the pads and around the toes, checking that the length of claws or toenails is such that the dog can move comfortably and can grip the ground. Most well-exercised dogs wear their nails down to correct length, but occasionally, due to an owner's indisposition, a dog can miss adequate exercising time. If the nails are too long they must be clipped. Not many owners like to do this, thinking they might hurt the dog, and prefer their veterinary surgeon to do this job. But providing you have the correct tool (your pet shop will sell you the one suited to your breed) it is a relatively simple operation. The cut must be made safely above the quick, if you cut into the quick it will bleed copiously and upset the dog. Finally, file down the nails and make them smooth. Check the pads for callousing, splits, and soreness, then in between for thorns and cysts. If you have to apply ointment make sure it is not poisonous as the dog will almost certainly lick it off when he is not being watched.

Always lift the dog's tail and examine the anal area. This should be perfectly clean, especially the glands themselves — there is one on either side of the anus. These glands sometimes need evacuating to remove sediment, which if left may cause abscesses. The method of evacuation is quite simple. Take a flat cotton-wool or cloth pad, place it under the dog's tail squeezing upwards and together with the fingers at the same time; this will expel the evil-smelling contents on to the pad, which can then be disposed of and the dog made comfortable.

Any canine health situation about which you are doubtful should be referred at once to your veterinary surgeon.

The bath

Normally, it is unnecessary to bath a grown dog much more than just occasionally. Certain breeds like Poodles and Fox Terriers need pre-show baths to bring them into exhibition brilliance, but the ordinary dog about the house fares better keeping himself clean. Puppies sometimes roll into noxious matter and need an urgent bath, but generally speaking bathing a youngster is an exercise best left until he is at least five months old.

Never bath a dog immediately following his meal. Avoid if possible very cold days if the animal has to go out of doors soon after his ablutions. Dogs are best bathed indoors and the whole operation should be conducted with the minimum of fuss. No dog should have unhappy memories of his first bath. He should be encouraged to enjoy the proceedings and the sense of well-being he gets with the final rub-down. It is a good plan to place a rubber mat on the floor of the bath so he does not slip and to protect both his eyes and ears from the smarting effect of the shampoo or soap. Smear around the eye-rims with a veterinary eye ointment or harmless mineral oil. Plug both ears with cotton-wool wads that have been rolled in petroleum jelly. This will prevent the water entering the inner ear. *Don't* forget to remove these and wipe over the eyes when bathtime is over.

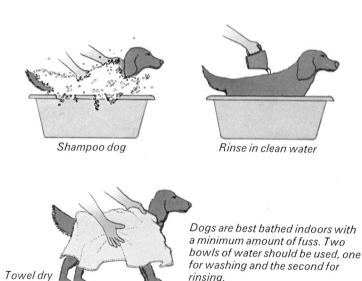

Shampoo dog

Rinse in clean water

Towel dry

Dogs are best bathed indoors with a minimum amount of fuss. Two bowls of water should be used, one for washing and the second for rinsing.

55

Make sure the room temperature is even. Have two baths ready, one, half filled with *warm,* not hot, water, the other, with cooler water for rinsing. There are good dog soaps and shampoos to be obtained from any pet store and one of these should be used. Some household soaps have an irritant effect on a dog's skin, and detergents or soaps with too high a soda-crystal content are quite unsuitable. Following the shampoo instructions, work the soap right down into the dog's undercoat and on to the skin, starting first at his rear end and leaving his head until last. Make sure that no soap gets into his eyes, causing irritation and probably some panic. Once the whole body has been covered, lift him into the rinsing bath and wash out every particle of soap. Try to complete the bath with this initial rinse so that any further douching or rinsing you do will serve to make doubly sure the animal is clean and free from soap, which if left will cloy and cause irritation. A few drops of vinegar placed in a large pitcher of cool water and poured slowly over the dog will ensure a perfect rinse.

Allow the dog to shake himself, then commence to dry him with the first of the three rough towels you should have ready : this will soak up surplus moisture left after the shake, the other towels being used to dry and rub down. Make sure you dry in and around the ears and eyes, under the tail, and between the toes. Towel down well the underbody and especially around the genitals and loins. If the weather is mild he can have a brief run round in the garden, but get him back indoors quickly and complete with a brisk towelling. Then start brushing and combing, as required.

Dealing with external parasites

Seldom does a dog go through life without picking up a flea or two. These parasites find the dog a good host, and, as they multiply alarmingly, it is important to keep a sharp eye out for infestation. Fleas' favourite haunts on the dog's body include the ears, back and sides of the neck, but more particularly around the root of the tail and upon the croup or back end of the spine. They cause the dog intense irritation, but they also leave the dog vulnerable to skin troubles and tapeworm. The dog flea is a great jumper as well as a fast mover along the dog's body : this is why any attack made on the parasite must be in the form of a 'blitzkrieg' rather than a slow, calculated move. Some owners prefer dipping the dog into one of the proprietary vermin dips that can be bought for the purpose. These are effective, but in the author's opinion should not be used too frequently in case the dog's skin should be an over-sensitive

The flea's favourite haunts on the body of a dog include the ears, back and sides of the neck, but particularly around the root of the tail and upon the croup or back end of the spine.

one. A good flea powder, obtainable from the local pet shop and *specifically prepared for dogs,* is probably best. Quick action with this will bemuse the fleas who can then be removed – together with their eggs—by employing a fine-toothed comb and standing the dog on newspaper or an old blanket, which can be burned with the fleas when the exercise is over. It is necessary to go right over the dog's skin and through every inch of his coat in an effort to locate every flea. Any left on the dog will soon start breeding and re-infest the animal. Much work and worry can be avoided by checking your dog for fleas and other parasites during his daily grooming.

Lice are often collected from grass and hay during the summer months. There are two kinds, the biting and the sucking lice, and they frequent all parts of the dog's body once they have become established. They are very small, often not much larger than half a pin head and their function is to bite and suck and cause intense irritation and anaemia, to young stock in particular. Both the lice and their nits (eggs) must be disposed of immediately they have been detected. A good proprietary powder dusted in, or similar de-lousing wash, will prove effective and this should be repeated in the case of the dusting powder on alternate days and about every eight days for the wash. Make sure that all bedding and surrounding material likely to harbour the pests is burned. It is also a necessary precaution to dust around corners and floor cracks with powder or disinfectant to make sure any lice that have escaped from the host have been exterminated.

A tick is particularly loathsome as it gorges itself upon the blood of its host and is capable of transmitting viral diseases and various toxic complaints. About the size of a small pea, it swells as it gorges, almost to the size of a haricot bean, changing in colour from browny-white to a purple. It buries its nose, through which it sucks, into the dog's skin and is very difficult to dislodge. It is best to remove it manually or with tweezers, although an effective method is to dab its body with a spot of turpentine: it will then let go its grip and can be lifted off. Rub over the spot where it has bitten with a smear of iodine. A dog will usually take on these parasites in summer months from the long grass adjoining field tracks; there the ticks wait to drop off on to unsuspecting hosts as they pass by. Some will live in cracks and crevices about the home, particularly in old furniture. It is important to disinfect places where it is thought they might be: there are various powders and disinfectants available for this purpose.

Harvest mites resemble red pepper, although their shape is reminiscent of the tick, already described. They burrow under the skin of the attacked host and are difficult to eradicate. Intense irritation is caused and they attack areas such as inside the thighs, between the toes, the soft parts of the underbelly and armpits, revealing their presence with an inflamed rash which blisters. They are prevalent in hot weather and the affected areas should be bathed with a reliable antiseptic lotion or dusted with a pesticide powder.

Biting louse *Sucking louse*

Flea

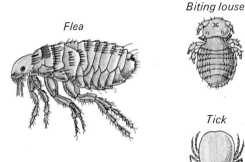

Tick

Mite

External parasites found on dogs

Breeding, mating, and whelping

Look at your bitch

If you own a pedigree breed, you may well be tempted to breed from your pet. Besides providing an absorbing interest, if there are children in your family, they will learn a lot from the process and will acquaint themselves, with the fascination of animal husbandry.

A breeder's aim is to produce an animal which is at least as good as the one he owns, better if possible. If he can achieve the latter then he will have done a worthwhile service to his breed and will feel a real sense of achievement. Unfortunately, few breeders possess what can be claimed as a sound working knowledge of genetics, but oddly enough many dog lovers do have 'an eye' for a dog. This instinct has held many in good stead in their time and enabled them to produce, by good assessment of mating pairs, some worthwhile stock.

Look first of all at your bitch. Is she good? Has she turned out as well as you expected? What have the experts said about her? Has she a good pedigree, a good strain? If you are a lucky owner then you can answer 'yes' to most of these questions and feel heartened in the thought that, having picked the right dog for her, you stand a fairly good chance of successful breeding. If she is just an average specimen with a fair share of faults and not from the pre-eminent bloodline in her breed, then your task is perhaps more difficult, but at least you have the right to try to improve upon her by careful selection of her mate. Provided you have a reasonably good bitch, who is sound both physically and temperamentally, never be persuaded to delay your hand at breeding. Too many people with a flair for breeding good dogs have been kept in the background by others in the 'fancy' who have told them not to breed because their bitch 'was not good enough'. An *average* bitch with type is good enough to breed from, providing you intend to improve upon her. The only ones to keep free from puppies are the type-less, vicious, and unsound. Bad mothers are a nuisance, too, but one can seldom find out their shortcomings without allowing them a litter first; although sometimes this vicissitude runs in families of bitches: this at least will forewarn you and allow you to take precautionary measures to protect the puppies and your interests.

If you plan to breed dogs regularly, as opposed to the single venture with just one pet bitch, then it is important to steel yourself to the hard-and-fast rule of keeping only good bitches in your

Rough Collie with her litter of pups

kennel. You will find, as you progress, that some dogs will become no more than 'passengers' to the kennel. This does not refer to the old and much-loved animal who has been in the home for many years and is part and parcel of the family. A pal of this kind deserves, and indeed should have, every care and comfort you can bestow upon it. The reference to 'passengers' refers to the *passé* breeding stock that sometimes accumulates in the kennel, serving no useful purpose and merely causing extra expense. You can serve such an animal better by finding it a good home somewhere: there it will receive individual attention (which you may well be unable to give it) and become a pet in its own right with a nice family. Much better for it this way than to let it finish its days in a kennel, enjoying human companionship for only very brief periods.

The pedigree

To many this is a mere piece of paper. People take it home when they buy their dog, put it in a safe place somewhere, and promptly forget about it. To you as a breeder, however, it is an important document. Remember, though, that a dog is only as good as its pedigree and no matter how superb and handsome she is to look at, if a bitch has in her blood some poor ancestry, this will fashion the shape and quality of her stock issue. Conversely, no pedigree is worth any more than the dog it refers to. You might have before you a pedigree full to the brim of champions – the best in the breed; but it means very little if your animal is a poor specimen. The ideal situation is to own a good-looking dog with a good-looking pedigree. From such a dog or bitch you will then stand a very reasonable chance of producing good puppies. It is important to study your bitch's pedigree. What stock has she behind her? Do her ancestors boast the prestige of a noted strain or are they mediocre in form and lacking note? Try to obtain the help of a person well steeped in the breed that interests you. He or she should know the dogs of the past twenty or more years, and will probably have judged most of them or at least watched them being judged from the ringside. He will know their stamp, remember their careers, their colours, sizes, and reputations. He will remember their faults too. It is odd how experts, even the unbiased ones, will recall faults more easily than good points. But you will want to know both and you must press for information on the dogs whose names appear on the piece of paper before you. If one man cannot supply enough information ask others, but refer only to people with good reputations themselves – people who can impart facts that are authentic, not mere guesswork or hearsay. Draft out your pedigree on a large piece of paper and beneath the name of every dog and bitch ancestor, in its own square, write in the data you have gleaned. Try to get details on *every* animal, even if it means writing to people long since out of the breed. You will usually find someone in the family who recalls the dog their sister, brother, or father owned and can tell you something about it; but do not forget to enclose a stamped, addressed envelope. From the facts you accumulate you should be able to form a perfect word picture of the ancestral qualities and faults behind your bitch, probably sufficient to ensure that when you come to select a stud dog for her you will at least be forearmed with knowledge that will enable you to avoid, in her puppies, any duplication of the bitch's faults capable of being passed on, often in double measure, to her progeny.

Pedigrees can usually be relied upon these days. In the very old days records of a dog's breeding would only have been kept casually, to say the least. In certain cases, such information was jealously guarded by owners and breeders, especially if the specimens involved were good ones. The pedigree was then thought more a 'secret formula' than a breeding record, to be used freely in an effort to improve subsequent generations.

Breeding methods
Line-breeding

This is the most popular system of breeding dogs today. It is quite simple, provided care is taken not to introduce stock that falls below standard quality. Line-breeding is really the mating of relatives, and entails the following crosses:

Grandson to Grand-dam
Grandsire to Grand-daughter
Cousin to Cousin

and includes the mating of aunts and nephews, uncles and nieces, and half-brothers to sisters. Briefly, it means that quite closely related animals can be mated, but *not* immediate relatives, such as brother and sister. In line-breeding the pedigrees of both mates should carry similar bloodlines, but it is not essential that they have all the same bloodlines, and a common ancestor may well appear twice in the last five generations. When assessing the pedigrees of both the dam and her prospective mate, as you will do in due course, it is often a good thing if you can detect one or two strong, vital lines to a dominant sire or dam whose type and quality you wish to aim for in the litter to be bred. Having found this, it is sometimes a good thing if the remaining parts of the pedigrees are not involved with effective bloodlines capable of counteracting, perhaps adversely, the effect of the ancestral sire or dam on whose type and characteristics you have set your sights. The method of line-breeding is a sound one, although you may well have to wait patiently for results, unlike in-breeding which, while faster, is fraught with greater dangers. Line-breeding takes a time to establish purity of strain, and once this point has been reached not a lot can be done to improve further while your own kennel stock is being employed in the programme of breeding. Then you will have to consider the introduction of fresh blood and, with care, you can maintain the purity you have achieved in your strain and inject it with a new lease of life.

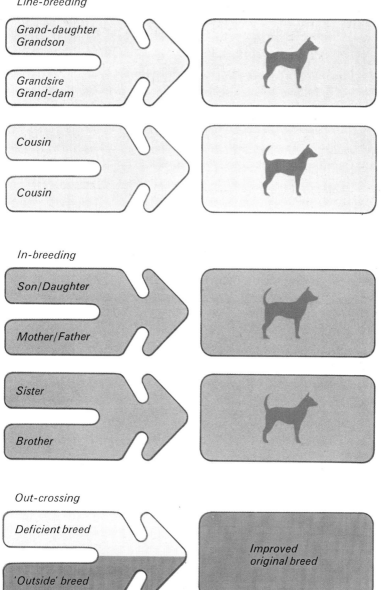

Line-breeding

Grand-daughter
Grandson

Grandsire
Grand-dam

Cousin

Cousin

In-breeding

Son/Daughter

Mother/Father

Sister

Brother

Out-crossing

Deficient breed

'Outside' breed

Improved
original breed

In-breeding

This is the mating of closely related dogs, i.e. son to mother, father to daughter, brother to sister. It should be done only in lines that are very strong, showing a high standard to type, health, soundness, and temperament. That these characteristics need to be perpetuated with each and every generation goes without saying and in-breeding will aid such dominance. Only really first-class material must be employed, and if you try in-breeding with lowly stock you will do no more than quickly 'fix' lowly points in your strain. The idea of in-breeding is to secure firmly the *good* points in your strain, but if your strain is liberally endowed with a number of indifferent features, then it will establish some of these for you too ! That is why only animals which fall into a category which can claim freedom from distinct defects can be permitted entry to the breeding programme. Rigorous culling of unwanted stock must take place prior to the planned furtherance of each generation. The breeder must be honest with himself, recognise where weaknesses exist in his stock, and only employ parental pairs that he knows in his heart can maintain the high standard of his kennel. If he fails in this assessment he is doomed to failure for the longer defects are permitted to exist the more time and effort will be needed to eradicate them, always with the very real possibility of degeneration creeping in to ruin the work of years.

Out-crossing

In serious dog breeding, the out-cross is today seldom employed. The system has its value when the out-cross employed is a dog that has some connection with the original strain, linked, perhaps, through a pre-potent line. In the old days, an out-cross was used to improve any deficiencies that might have existed in a working strain. For example, once Lord Orford put a Bulldog to Greyhounds because it was felt the latter needed stamina. Whether such a move proved worthwhile we do not know, but the only out-cross system of any value is when an outside dog can improve the health and type of a strain that has deteriorated, perhaps due to slapdash breeding. Some folk believe that an out-cross dog can improve, invigorate, even produce big winners from a negative strain. This is not so, and if by chance such a big winner did arise from the strain it would be no more than a 'sport', which is a good specimen, but without anything worthwhile in its blood, and probably incapable of passing on even mediocre qualities in his issue.

If an out-cross must be employed, and very often in far-flung districts where members of a breed are really sparse and the bitch owner has little or no choice, this can occur, then at least make sure that both parents-to-be are sound and healthy in all departments before allowing any union. If, however, an out-cross is planned with a specific purpose in mind then make sure that the dog has factors that render him at least competent to correct any in-bred faults that the bitch possesses. It must be remembered that a sire endowed with such factors and able to rectify the faults is a much better agent as an out-cross than a dog with such strong and dominant bloodlines that he can completely submerge the fault, yet cause to arise to the surface some bad feature, never suspected. The breeder must be prepared in his out-cross results for an uneven litter, and perhaps experience some disappointment at the apparent lack of success of the exercise. Very often the good points expected will appear in the second generation — i.e. the grandchildren — rather than with the initial progeny.

The bitch

You have now to decide whether your own bitch (assuming you have one) is to be employed in your breeding programme or whether you intend to buy one. Many people believe that the female is the more important of a mating pair, at least as far as determining the quality of her puppies is concerned. It is an acknowledged fact that whereas it is easier to assess a dog's abilities at stud by virtue of the greater number of offspring he produces, a bitch's progeny must necessarily be much fewer. Consider objectively, therefore, the female lines as far as possible, because tail-female (which is the dam's dam's dam — or family) is more important than tail-male (which is the sire's sire's sire — or Line).

This means that you *must* have a good bitch if you are to breed really *good* puppies. It has been pointed out in earlier pages that you are entitled to use any sound, healthy, and reasonably typical bitch for breeding, in a fair effort to improve on her particular virtues through the medium of her puppies. If show stock is your intent, then you will need to aim a little higher than a mediocre bitch as your producer. Obviously, with a good bitch, you might breed some very good puppies with quite an ordinary stud dog, but even a successful sire may well fail to produce anything but ordinary stock from a plain bitch.

You should buy the best bitch you can afford. This does not

mean a bitch has to be expensive, but if you get the opportunity to purchase a young female of obvious worth at a fair price she may well repay you twenty-fold. Seek an adult bitch of not more than twenty months or a well-grown puppy as free from faults in her type and construction as possible. Always employ either a knowledgeable companion to advise you or put your trust in a reputable kennel of your chosen breed. Make sure you know the breed Standard before you start negotiating and put in a lot of time at major shows (especially championship events) where your fancy is on display and being judged. Listen to the competent authorities talk about the exhibits and the judging results. See whether you can follow their lines of thought for yourself. Make sure that the people you listen to know what they are talking about: too many people in dogs 'think' they know. Many years experience in a breed qualifies *most* people to speak reliably about the dog, but length of time in a breed does not necessarily make an expert. Some enthusiasts can learn in five years what it takes others thirty years to assimilate.

Knowing something of your breed, you will commence your search for a bitch who is typical, sound, and healthy. She must be robust and have adequate width of pelvis to ensure that she is well equipped for the rigours of puppy bearing. It is important, too, that she be quite feminine – a doggy bitch is objectionable. Check her teeth to see that she has the required jaw formation for her breed and that her teeth and gums are in good condition. Watch also for signs of nervousness, but bear in mind that many young females are ill at ease in the company of strangers. The

Boxer Bitch

matter should be followed up for your own satisfaction, just as you should do with any other feature of your intended purchase. Take each 'worry' as it comes, eliminating them one by one, not only by judicious questioning but by actual physical handling of the animal.

The dog

As the dog you are likely to use with your bitch will probably belong to someone else, you are free to take your time finding him. *Never* use an untried dog at stud. You might fancy your chances as an assessor of canine virtues in the blood, but you will need to be little more than a magician to hit the jackpot with such a sire. It is better to let someone else try him first — then you can look at his puppies, taking into consideration their dam, and judge better his qualities.

Always choose a stud dog on his record as a stud dog. This means his 'get' or progeny brand him as good or bad at the job. A show dog with all the cards and ribbons a winner can muster in his brief term on the show bench, should never influence you. Much of his winning can be worthless, sometimes in classes where the competition is sparse, or mediocre. Many a champion has won his third and deciding challenge certificate at an out-of-the-way championship show, which is invariably poorly supported by the usual show-going crowd. Plenty of first prizes are very nice, but they do nothing more than tell you that the dog is probably a good specimen in himself, but it does not tell you what good he can do to his breed. The 'good' that comes from a dog is in what he can produce.

Boxer Dog

Do not think that because your bitch is deficient in one department or another that her fault or faults can be corrected at once by putting her to a dog who is strong in the features that she lacks. The first things you must make yourself aware of are the weak points in her make-up; unless you do this and freely accept her faults you will never correct them. Any fault can be bred out of a strain given time, care, and calculation. But, naturally, you have to guard against breeding in other faults, hitherto unknown in the strain, while you are dispersing those you know about!

Look for a dog who is really a handsome, upstanding, masculine, and quite typical specimen, conforming closely to his breed Standard. Find this kind of sire and then look around at the litters he has produced, preferably young sons and daughters of his who have reached the yearling stage. Assuming they look good and that some are already winning around the show circuits, then you may have the dog you seek — provided, of course, he lines up satisfactorily with your bitch in the important matter of their respective breeding. Take *his* pedigree and do with it what you did with your bitch's: fill in the description of all those of his ancestors you can acquire facts about, then, with his dossier placed above that of your bitch's, compare them point to point. If line-breeding is to be your plan of campaign, you must find, within at least the fourth generation, the name of a beautiful breed specimen worth breeding to, and whose name appears as a common denominator to both pedigrees.

You must make sure that the stud dog possesses an ideal temperament. If he has won his position under judges specialising in your chosen breed, it is highly probable that this characteristic will have been determined well, for most breed fanciers know what to look for and realise the need for maintaining a sound temperament. A pedigree breed lacking true breed temperament is only 'half' a dog and certainly not one to be used with the intention of building a strain in your kennel.

The mating

Soon your bitch will be ready for taking on maternal duties, which means that not only should she be of reasonably mature physical proportions, but past her first 'heat', or season: she will be about fifteen months of age or older. You will presumably have a fairly good idea as to when her next heat is due. It is best to advise the stud dog owner that you propose using his dog and then later when she nears her time of season give him adequate warning

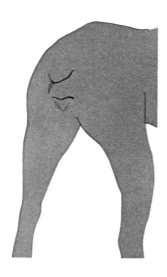

Vulva of a bitch before heat

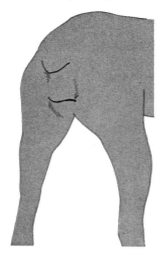

The vulva swollen ready for mating, which can occur on the tenth to fourteenth day of oestrus.

of the date. Once she begins to show 'colour', a bright blood discharge at the mouth of the vulva (which will have swollen a little a few days earlier, followed by an intermediary pinkish secretion), you will know she is shortly to be ready for mating. The term is usually between ten and fourteen days from the commencement of the initial discharge, by which time all signs of blood will have dispersed, although the oestrum or season itself usually lasts about three weeks.

Bitches vary enormously in their preferred day for mating. Some will receive a dog any time between the tenth and fourteenth day, even a little later, others seem to like more specific days. These have to be catered for or you will never get them mated, and if you learn by experience that your bitch is one to be mated on, say, the eleventh day of her heat, then you must ensure that you book her to the stud dog for just that day – no other will do. Another type of bitch, and this sort is rather a nuisance, becomes ripe for mating over a very short term, sometimes for only a few hours in the season. It is not always easy to catch them at this time and the answer seems to be that both dog and bitch be kennelled in adjoining runs. Then, when the bitch is ready for the dog, she will indicate this in the usual manner and the dog can be introduced at once. Such an arrangement is rather trying to the stud dog who will be 'teased' to his disadvantage, perhaps for many hours, before he can get the bitch. Needless to add, not many stud-dog owners like bitches of this kind, and if you have such a female you might find extra fees and/or charges to pay for the inconvenience she causes.

It is usual for the bitch to visit the dog, although some stud-dog owners do not mind doing it the other way round, so long as you pay fares, etc. Often enough it suits a bitch better to be mated on her own territory and the job is then accomplished with minimum delay. If you take your charge to the dog, try to arrange it so that the union can be effected fairly early in the morning, and always try to accompany your bitch to the dog. No bitch should be transported a long distance to arrive in strange surroundings and find herself involved with a dog whom she may well not like. She will almost certainly be in a very nervous state, being in season, and a bitch in distressed condition is liable to 'miss', even following a good mating, and this means you will have to wait at least another six months before you can try again. Further, if you are present at the scene of the mating you can come away feeling satisfied that the dog in use was the one of your choice and that you saw things through from start to finish.

Ensure that both animals have had a free run around with ample time to attend to their natural functions. Usually if the stud dog is an experienced animal he will lose little time in making overtures. It is best to have both dogs on their respective leashes during the introduction; this will allow the bitch to be edged away from him if she grabs at him in annoyance. It may seem prudent to present her to him rear end first, when his attentions will soon excite her. If you and the stud dog owner feel that the pair will get on well together they can be released and watched closely as they run free. Never leave a mating pair unattended in spite of listening to some breeders who seem to prefer a 'natural' mating. This entails dog and bitch being left alone to conduct affairs unaided and in their own way. Sometimes the pair do effect copulation without much ado and, of course, this is ideal, but, more often than not, there is a skirmish or two before the dog can enter the bitch and even when entry has been effected and a 'tie' made, a fidgety and impatient bitch can do a dog and herself a good deal of harm.

The stud dog's natural instinct will make him take the initiative and mount the bitch from behind; he will at once begin to thrust at her and an experienced male will soon enter. Once this has been seen, the stud-dog owner should come behind him and steady the dog squarely and firmly against the bitch's rear while you should hold your bitch's head firmly on either side of her neck. This will not only give her confidence and re-assurance, but prevent her from swinging round at the crucial moment and trying to dislodge the dog. If matters proceed well the 'tie' will

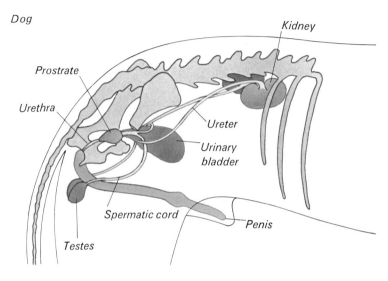

Dog

Kidney

Prostrate

Urethra

Ureter

Urinary bladder

Spermatic cord

Penis

Testes

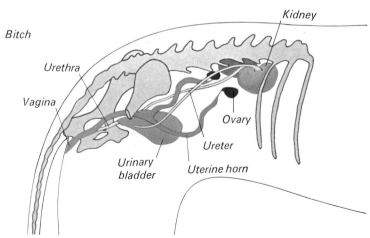

Bitch

Kidney

Urethra

Vagina

Ovary

Ureter

Urinary bladder

Uterine horn

soon be achieved, and this will mean that seminal fluid is being deposited and that a proper mating can be assumed. The 'tie', to explain the term quite briefly, is caused by a bulb situated in the dog's penis. It becomes engorged with blood as the penis erects and swells to several times its normal size. It is then held securely in position by the sphincter muscle of the bitch's vagina, thereby locking both animals together. It is best, if this can be managed, to turn the pair tail-to-tail for their own comfort while the mating continues. This can be achieved by lifting the dog carefully so that his forelegs can be brought off the bitch's back and put on the ground beside her. Then, taking one of the dog's hind legs, lift it gently over the bitch's back, at the same time swivelling him round and away from her. This movement will culminate in their heads pointing different ways, but the pair will remain 'tied'. Such unions last from a few minutes up to even an hour and a half, but the usual time is twenty minutes. The mating pair should be supervised until they come apart from each other, as towards the end of the union either or both animals will commence to fidget. Once parted, the dog should be removed from the bitch's presence and his personal comfort attended to by ensuring that his sheath has returned to the correct position over the penis. The bitch should be dried over at the rear and both animals can then be allowed to drink, and also fed if necessary a little later. If you notice that seminal fluid appears to have been spilled, do not worry. It is likely that much more spermatozoa than seems wasted will have been deposited into the bitch's vagina, and when it is remembered that in one mating many million of sperms are released, the chances of a 'miss' (failure to conceive) are slight. This presumes of course, that all other factors are good and normal.

Some breeders prefer to have their bitch mated twice by the stud dog. This seems to give them added confidence that the bitch will 'take' and prove successful in having puppies. With a stud dog in regular use, this is quite unnecessary if the initial mating was a good one. But with a dog never before used at stud, an elderly male, or one seldom used, it can prove a wise precaution: the second union should follow the first within twenty hours. Most stud dogs are vital animals and things seldom go wrong if their mating has been handled expertly. It is often a good plan to get a young dog stud 'shown the ropes' at, say ten months of age by a matron bitch whose manner at mating time will give him confidence. Once he has had a stud job, then it is best to let him rest until he can have a second bitch at, say, fifteen months of age. Then from two years onwards he can start his stud career in earnest. However, watch him all the time to ensure that he maintains good condition: he will need plenty of fresh, raw-meat feeding, ample protein, and so on. Never expect too much sense at mating time from a dog who has been celibate for three years; often such a dog has no idea what to do when he is introduced to a bitch in full heat. Such dogs, if they are worth using, may need a good deal of re-assurance and perhaps manipulative assistance in order to effect a proper mating.

Pre-natal care

Some breeds do not easily reveal to the eye that they are in whelp until quite near the normal term of gestation, which is sixty-three days. However, it is very important to start preparations for the hoped-for litter, and the bitch's prime condition must be her owner's first thought. She must be exercised quite normally every day and groomed in the usual way, but guided well away from any activity that might prove harmful. The bitch will need worming perhaps, and this can be discussed with your veterinary surgeon, although there are many reliable home remedies on the market. The vet will also advise on injections. The modern bitch is beset with a number of infections which fall mainly into the streptococcal and staphylococcal categories. Your professional man will know what to do to avoid fading puppies – whelps that eventually die after a miserable week of life – also absorption, when no puppies arrive after what appears to be a normal pregnancy. These are of course dangers that you might never become involved with.

Some breeds produce large litters – sometimes as many as a round dozen, but from five to ten is normal to most breeds. This means that not only the dam, but also the whelps she is carrying, need building up. This can be achieved not only with good and perhaps improved feeding, but also with extra nourishment, including calcium phosphate sources, and especially plenty of milk.

Prepare a whelping box or place for her. If using a box make sure that it is sufficiently big and roomy. If she has the maximum number of puppies, then space will be tight. The box should allow room for the dam to lie down in comfort with her puppies. The 'pig-rail' will permit a small puppy some protection from being squashed by its mother, and the front can be let down for easy access and exit if required. A piece of laundered hessian is ideal for affixing to the bottom of the box, but until the bitch has had her puppies and has settled down with them, it is as well to let her do the actual whelping either on the bare board of the base or on newspapers, which are ideal, for they can be gathered up and disposed of at will, and replaced immediately with clean ones. The bitch should be introduced to her new quarters about ten days before she is due to whelp. Do not expect her to react kindly to the suggestion a few hours before her litter arrives; she will have enough to think about at this time without having the distraction of a strange bed. Never use straw or blankets in the whelping box. The puppies crawl out of sight underneath these and are in danger of being squashed if the bitch cannot see them.

Make sure that you have informed your veterinary surgeon of the expected date of whelping. You might need him in an emergency and he will then be ready for any urgent call.

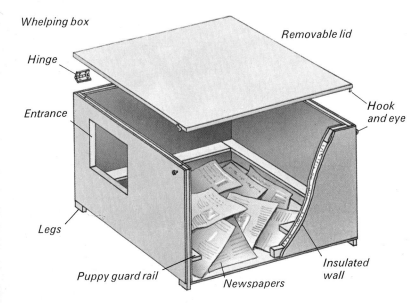

Whelping box

Removable lid

Hinge

Entrance

Hook and eye

Legs

Puppy guard rail

Newspapers

Insulated wall

The whelping

As the time for having her puppies draws closer, you will observe the bitch becomes steadily less relaxed, until just prior to actual whelping she may show real signs of restlessness, even agitation. This usually involves turning around on herself, sudden 'braking' when moving, and clear indication of worry, more evident in a maiden bitch than one who has experienced it all before. These symptoms often continue for two or three days prior to the actual day of whelping, by which time her temperature, which is normally 38.5°C will have dropped to 37.7°C or 36.4°C when she is about to deliver her young. A cautious breeder will find this a good and safe guide warning him that labour is about to commence.

The bitch will probably refuse all meals in the early stages of pre-labour. Just prior to whelping she will fall into a deep sleep which will set her up well for the coming ardours of giving birth. It should be arranged, when you see her in this state, that she is left well alone and not in any way annoyed by strangers or other dogs, even those known to her. The room temperature should not be less than 21°C.

When the bitch awakens she will probably be ready to start her labours and this will be intimated when she scratches at the floor of her box and by her general restlessness. You should have ready by you in the whelping room a number of first-aid items, including:

a Paper tissues.
b Surgical lint cut into 10 in. squares.
c Sharp, probe-pointed surgical scissors, sterilized.
d Surgical cotton, cut to pieces about 6 in. long.
e Antiseptic/disinfectant.
f Petroleum jelly in tube or jar.
g Supply of cotton wool.
h Odd pieces of clean washed towelling or face flannels.
i Hot-water bottle (old-fashioned stone variety best) covered with cloth or sock for protection.
j Feeding bottle or pipette.
k Kettle of water, readily plugged in to mains or on gas.
l Brandy, small teaspoon. This is either for bitch, her puppies (in which case absolute minimal measures to be given), or yourself!
m Plenty of old newspapers.
n Basin.

Obviously you can make your own selection of these requisites, but the purpose of the exercise is that you should be ready with the things you want rather than having to search around for them at a time when your presence may well be better employed alongside your bitch.

The bitch will soon commence to strain, the periods of labour becoming more frequent as she gets nearer to delivering her first puppy. If you think it prudent, offer her a little warm milk. She may or may not take it, but it does so often have the effect of hastening the arrival of her first-born. It is usually better to leave her well alone, do not feed her, do not talk to her, just let her get on with the job. If everything proceeds properly, a small water-filled bag will appear at the mouth of the vulva. This is a sort of cushion or buffer which will protect the on-coming puppy when it greets the out-side world. The bitch's muscular contractions will eventually rend the bag, the puppy soon following in a membraneous sac, head first. The bitch, with vigorous licking, will break the sac, releasing the puppy together with a good deal of fluid, which will be soaked-up by the newspapers lining the whelping box. The puppy, following its buffeting by the bitch's tongue will soon commence to breathe, even squeak with some apparent peevish-ness. It will be attached by its umbilical cord to the afterbirth (placenta) and the bitch will instinctively sever the cord close to the whelp's navel with a sharp nip. If she seems unable or disinclined to conduct this simple operation it must be done for her. Take one of the ready prepared short lengths of surgical thread and tie it tightly round the umbilical cord, about an inch up from the puppy's navel, then cut the cord with the sterilized scissors about one inch above the thread tie you have made. Sometimes the bitch will devour the afterbirth and if this happens, well and good, it will do her no harm as it is a perfectly natural thing for her to do. If she does not eat it then dispose of it for her. Sometimes the afterbirth remains in the womb when it will have to be withdrawn gently or it may decompose and cause a septic condition. The withdrawal can be effected by drawing carefully and directly on the hanging cord until it is quite free from the bitch's body.

Sometimes a puppy is stubborn in coming through or its position seems an abnormal one, then it may need assistance. Breech births are easy enough, i.e. when the feet or rear end is presented first, in which case the part to be seen is gripped gently with one of the towel pieces you have ready and the puppy is withdrawn without ado. Make sure, if you have to do this, that you do it with all speed if the bag is already broken, but take care that you do not squeeze the whelp's body in your anxiety. Try to effect the with-drawal in rhythm with the natural straining of the dam, but deft speed at such a time is of great importance. If you feel doubtful as to your ability at such a task, then it is better to call in your veterinary surgeon when the need arises.

The bitch will usually sleep or doze between deliveries and this should be encouraged as she is gathering her energies in this way. Usually, if she has managed to deliver three puppies without trouble the rest will follow automatically, the intervals between each one frequently varying quite considerably. As she progresses you should try to make an opportunity for clearing up, as the bulk of water which is released at every birth makes quite a lot of mess. Once the bitch seems to have finished, try to get her to go outside and relieve herself, and give her a bowl of warm milk to encourage this. Once outside you can commence a quick tidy-up, putting the puppies into a basket nearby and disposing at once of the soiled newspapers. Check every puppy for its sex and make sure no abnormalities exist. Provided you are satisfied that there are no more puppies to come you can leave the bitch to her own devices for a while, but if you are in doubt then the opinion of your veterinary surgeon should be sought, although once a bitch has settled down and the puppies are sucking away merrily at her there is very little chance of further arrivals and all should be well.

The most useful size of litter is about five. Some bitches, although able to cope with more, will make the best of seven, and such a number is enough for a dam. You may well have a larger litter than this, in which case a foster mother will prove the prudent thing. Foster mothers are often advertised in the canine press, and certain kennels specialise in supplying good clean bitches (often Collies) for the purpose. If you have, say, a litter of nine puppies you can put five on to the natural dam, four on to the Collie, and you will get maximum results. However, for the first four days it is best to keep the entire litter on your bitch, for then they will all get the benefit of her initial milk flow, which is of prime value to them. Make sure that every puppy is given a fair share of the feeding. The inguinal teats are most plenteous in their supply: these are the larger teats in the lower regions and you should make sure that each puppy is placed down here in his turn and watched so that he is not pushed off by greedier members of the litter. In the initial stages the bitch can be fed with a sustaining drink of warm milk to which a teaspoonful of glucose or a dessertspoonful of honey has been added. She should have plenty of milk to drink as this will aid her own milk supply.

Post-whelping problems

Eclampsia
This is a common occurrence after whelping, although it can happen shortly before a bitch delivers her puppies. It is a sort of milk fever and brings on restlessness and nervousness, accompanied by panting. The condition is brought about by a deficiency of calcium and vitamin D. The matter can be rectified with injections of calcium. Keep an eye on the dam and puppies every hour after whelping. Eclampsia can occur even three or four weeks after the date of the puppies' arrival and the danger period is not over until after weaning has been completed.

Aglactia
This is lack of milk and it is a condition quite common in bitches today. The dam suddenly acquires a high temperature and this prevents her milk passing through the teats to her puppies; she panics and the puppies make their displeasure quite audible! The condition persists as a rule for two to three days, which is rather worrying as milk flow in the initial stages is important. During this period the milk contains colostrum, which is not only a mild laxative, but is also highly nourishing, being well endowed with protein. It may also act as an antibiotic in the first few weeks of the puppy's life. Consequently the fact that its effect can be lost to the puppy is a worrying one.

A bitch will often improve after just a few hours of suffering this distressing condition, and she can be helped by continually pressing the puppies on to her teats, but if this proves of no avail, call in the veterinary surgeon. He will inject the bitch, thereby reducing her temperature, and once returned to normal body heat the milk will flow normally and the puppies feed and thrive happily.

Metritis
This is a condition usually due to the retention of the last-born puppy's placenta in the dam's womb, although it can be caused by even small particles of membrane which have been left behind. There is often an unpleasant septic discharge from the vulva and the bitch will appear in considerable discomfort, the milk flow being disrupted. Inflammation of the uterus is usually noted about a week after the whelping and the bitch's temperature and pulse rate will be high; urgent attention to the matter is important and the veterinary surgeon will have to act in order to save her.

Naturally, a bitch in this state will be unable to care for her puppies properly and the entire litter will have to be removed and either put to a foster dam or hand-reared.

Hand-rearing

This is by no means an easy task. It requires immense patience and the person doing it needs to be dedicated. The entire litter has to be fed as one, no individual puppy (unless he is a weakling) can be treated differently from his brothers and sisters. The weakling may need extra attention, although, frankly, if the litter to be hand-reared is but a day or so old and there is a weakling among them, it is probably better and kinder to painlessly destroy it. 'Lactol', or a similar proprietary brand, is a good substitute for bitch's milk, although there is no *true* substitute for the real thing. Instructions as to hand-rearing will be found on the canister, and great care should be taken to ensure that these are followed. It is just as important to keep to precise quantities of food as to exact times of feeding. Temperature of the food is another feature of vital importance and fresh food is necessary at every meal-time. There are a number of ways of administering the food to a small puppy, but care must be taken neither to overfeed nor to feed too fast. Keep the cup of 'Lactol' mixture in a bowl of warm water so that

Hand-reared puppies can be fed with Lactol mixture. Care should be taken to ensure that the correct temperature is maintained throughout the feeding by occasionally standing the cup in a bowl of hot water.

the temperature of the food can be maintained: this will ensure that when the last puppy in the litter comes to be fed, his food will be at the same correct temperature as when the first member was fed. A good guide as to whether the youngsters are being fed properly and are content can be taken from their attitude: happy puppies will settle down to sleep after they have been fed and cleaned-up, unsettled youngsters will cry incessantly and pass motions which instead of being of a firm porridge-like consistency and brown in colour, are loose and yellow. Such a sign is sufficient to warn the hand-rearer that the mixture he is feeding the puppies is too strong and needs diluting. The youngsters should be weighed daily and exact records kept, and each one examined closely to ensure its even development.

Once a puppy has been fed, wipe his face and especially his nose and lips with a swab of damp cotton wool. This will remove any milk that has settled there following his feed and will prevent the waste from congealing. The dam, if she were present, would lick the puppies clean, and lick and buffet them a little around their genitals and rear parts to induce urination and the passing of motions. This action must be dealt with artificially, however, and this can be done by soaking a wad of cotton wool in *warm* water and stroking the genitals gently. Once the motions have been passed, smear a little petroleum jelly around the anus and penis or vulva, as the case may be. No puppy should be allowed to remain constipated: in one so young this can prove fatal. If any youngster fails to pass its main motion following his meal, grease a veterinary thermometer and insert it fractionally into the rectum. This will invariably cause the required motion.

It is a good idea to install an infra-red lamp when you are maintaining an orphan litter deprived of its dam's body warmth. These lamps are freely available from the better pet stores or can be seen advertised in the canine press. An infra-red lamp should be set to produce a constant temperature of between 24°C–27°C, at least for the first three days. After this, the heat can be reduced to 16°C, but this must be done gradually and is achieved by raising the lamp a little each day. It is important to make sure that the lamp is suspended safely from the ceiling with no chance of it falling upon the puppies in their box or basket below. A dull-emitter bulb should be used, this being considered harmless to the youngsters' eyes when they open them about ten days after birth. Place a wire guard round the lamp reflector to give added security, in case a bulb should break loose and fall.

In spite of the time you will spend in hand-rearing and the sleep you cannot fail to lose in the process, you will experience a great and lasting satisfaction when the job is complete and you will realise how wonderfully fit and well are the litter of puppies you *might* have lost.

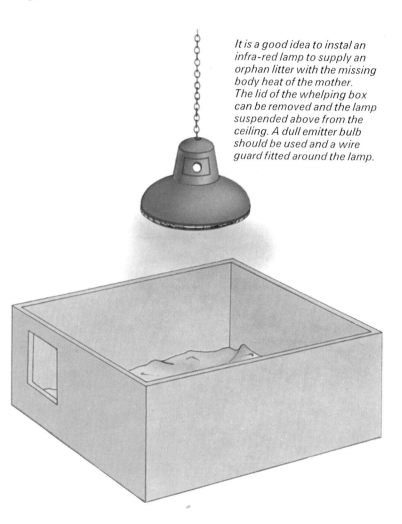

It is a good idea to instal an infra-red lamp to supply an orphan litter with the missing body heat of the mother. The lid of the whelping box can be removed and the lamp suspended above from the ceiling. A dull emitter bulb should be used and a wire guard fitted around the lamp.

Diseases and common ailments

A well-fed and cared-for dog, properly exercised and adequately inoculated, should be every owner's aim. Good rearing from puppyhood is the best investment against illness. It also allows veterinary bills to be kept low, and although few, if any, dogs go through life without at least some sickness or disease that needs professional attention, it is the duty of every dog owner to acquaint himself with the possible symptoms of canine sickness, especially of the various diseases in the virus field. There are also many common every-day complaints and ailments.

Virus diseases

These include Distemper, seldom heard of today due to the success of modern veterinary medicine. If it occurs it is usually between the ages of three and eighteen months, although a dog can catch it any time. It is normally indicated by loss of appetite, husky cough, and extreme lassitude, discharges from the eyes, and diarrhoea. Temperature can rise to over 38.9°C, at which point the veterinary surgeon should be in complete charge. The worst part of this disease is the aftermath: Chorea; this is a nervous disorder and shows itself when the dog is seemingly cured. Chorea is not an easy condition to correct. Effective immunisation is available against Distemper.

Hard pad

This is a form of Encephalitis and appears as an off-shoot from Distemper, being more serious than that disease. The symptoms are similar, and in fact the two diseases are sometimes confused. It is termed Hard Pad because, occasionally, the patient's nose will become encrusted and the pads of the feet harden and thicken. It is a disease which can prove fatal, but fortunately it is understood and can be dealt with effectively by a qualified veterinarian, providing prompt action is taken.

Hepatitis

Known as Canine Virus Hepatitis or Rubarth's Disease. Very infectious, it attacks liver and blood vessels, inducing jaundice. The temperature can rise to 40°C, with intense sleepiness, loss of appetite, diarrhoea, and vomiting. If experienced in the bitch it can affect her reproductive powers. Early action is essential if death is to be avoided. An excellent vaccine is available.

Leptospirosis (Leptospiral Jaundice)

These are two forms: Leptospiral *canicola* and *L. icterohaemo-rhagia*. The former attacks the kidneys, the virus infection coming from the urine of an infected dog. The latter attacks the liver and comes from the urine of infected rats. It is the more virulent of the two. Symptoms of Leptospiral infection are the usual ones of high temperature, sickness, diarrhoea, and extreme tiredness. There is a danger of lasting damage to the kidneys, even after an apparent cure.

Vaccination covers both types of Leptospirosis, but make sure the kennel or dog's quarters are scrupulously clean and any rats in the area eliminated.

Rabies ('Hydrophobia')

A very serious condition. The disease is a viral one. It comes from the saliva of an animal already infected. This means that a rabid dog *can* infect another dog (or a person) by biting. The saliva from an infected dog will probably cause rabies if it makes contact with an open wound.

The most noticeable symptom in the early stages is a distinct change of character in the dog. A friendly creature may become snappy and reserved and prefer his own company. The bark will vary in its note or pitch. He may howl or whine continuously and in the later stages completely reject water. This is due to muscular paralysis of the throat.

There is no known antidote and the disease – in animals or humans – is invariably fatal.

Ailments

ABNORMALITIES. The common abnormalities found at birth are Cleft Palate and Hare Lip. They are not uncommon malformations and can be detected in a new-born puppy by the way it holds open its mouth. Such puppies are unable to feed from their dam and usually fade and die. It is better to put them down at once.

ANAL GLANDS. These glands are situated on either side of the anus, and with correct feeding and normal motions they give little trouble. However, at times they become clogged with waste matter and often infected, causing the animal considerable discomfort. The dog so affected will drag his rear end along the ground and give every indication of the irritation. To treat, stand the dog on a bench at manageable level. Take a fair-sized pad of cotton wool or lint in one hand and raise the dog's tail with the other. Place the pad firmly over the glands and press, squeezing inwards and

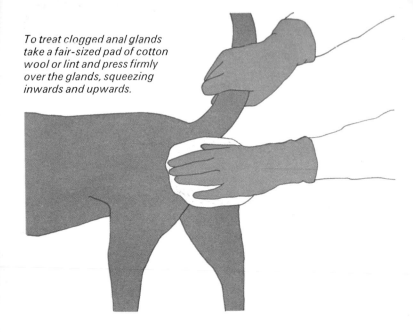

To treat clogged anal glands take a fair-sized pad of cotton wool or lint and press firmly over the glands, squeezing inwards and upwards.

upwards. The offending matter will be expelled from the glands and your dog will regain his comfort. If the condition is a long-standing one keep an eye open for abscesses and if any are indicated consult your veterinary surgeon.

CONSTIPATION. The symptoms are obvious and the treatment simple. Faulty diet, especially starchy food, is the main cause of this complaint, and green vegetables should be introduced to the feed at once. Often, too much biscuit meal and insufficient meat and vegetable juices is the cause, the motions being hard and pale in colour. If the condition persists, a teaspoonful of liquid paraffin will prove effective as a laxative or a good proprietary medicine can be administered to advantage. Increase the dog's exercise in an effort to tone him up.

CYSTS. Your first indication of these may be when you see the dog continually licking between his toes and pads. Cysts may also occur over the body area, and quite apart from their unsightly appearance, they cause the dog considerable discomfort. Some veterinary surgeons will cut them out, but the main cause seems to be a faulty diet and it is better to remove the *cause* of the cysts.

What might appear to be a form of cyst commonly occurs in mid-summer, when grass spears and the awns of wild meadow barley enter the soft skin between the dog's toes. Particles of flint from newly tarred roads may also be responsible. In such cases remove the offending object with tweezers and bathe the parts with a warm boracic solution or similar. Gravel or road tar adhering to the pads can be removed by holding the dog's foot in a bowl of turpentine or methylated spirit. Make sure afterwards that no trace of these spirits remain for the animal to lick.

DIARRHOEA. When a dog is seen to have this condition you should treat the matter seriously and make immediate efforts to bind the motions. Take the animal off meat at once, confining his feed to milky meals possibly with some arrowroot additive. The patient can return to meat meals within two or three days, when the condition has been corrected.

EARS. Rough-edged ears are a nuisance and unsightly. When neglected, the outer edges become serrated and unpleasantly dry to touch. A good remedy is a mild hair tonic worked into the affected area, left to dry then shampooed off. Treated twice a week for a month a cure should be effected, but take care the inner ear is protected during application.

EYES. If your dog has running, watery eyes and this symptom is not associated with others which might indicate something more serious, it is probably a case of simple conjunctivitis, a condition which can prove stubborn, or at least recurring. Wipe the eyes clean then insert a globule of a suitable eye ointment.

DISCHARGES. Any form of discharge should have prompt attention, as it will imply some form of infection. The usual forms are:

Discharge from eyes (referred to above).

Discharge from nose. Any sign of mucus issuing from the nostrils could indicate the beginnings of viral infection and the dog should be referred to your veterinary surgeon without delay. However, a dog perspires through his nose and a constant and clear dampness is usually a sign of good health.

Discharge from penis. This is known as Balanitis. It is fairly common in a dog whose activities in the stud field have been curbed or are non-existent. Douche beneath the sheath a mild solution of antiseptic in a proportion of 1:5 in tepid water. Treat night and morning until the condition has been cleared.

Discharge from mouth. Halitosis often indicates an excess of tartar on or behind the teeth. Mild cases can be cured by giving the dog a large marrow bone or hard biscuit to chew, but severe cases require action with a special tool, obtainable from most pet stores; this is used to scrape away the tartar. Sometimes the mouth region of a dog will smell due to ulceration in the folds or wrinkles about his mouth and lips. This is more common in the dog of advanced years and should be treated with a weak solution of hydrogen peroxide applied to the ulcerated area on a pad of cotton wool.

Discharge from teats. A bitch in the post-nursing period may suffer congestion in the teat region, especially with the inguinal teats, which are the larger ones at the rear. These become inflamed and often cause abscesses which prove intensely irritating. The congestion itself is due to excess milk supply, probably because the breeder commenced early weaning of his puppies. When this is noted, the teats should be gently 'milked' by hand and the bitch's fluid intake restricted. Admittedly, such milking may well encourage the milk supply to build up, but this is usually absorbed later by the growing puppies. There are drugs available to offset the condition, but natural methods are better employed.

Discharge from vagina. This is common in a bitch just after whelping. She should be checked to ensure that she has not retained any afterbirth, as in this case a septic condition could develop. The veterinary surgeon will know what to do to offset such a discharge and an injection will usually put matters right. However, a daily check should be made on the bitch to ensure normal progress. When a bitch is in 'season' there is a flow of blood from the vagina which follows a light-coloured discharge. This is normal and should cause no concern. However, after mating, should the bitch recommence the flow in an abnormal manner, she should be professionally examined, as anything unusual about the oestral flow requires attention. Some bitches continue their menstrual flow for a day or so in mild form after mating and this has no significance.

Discharge from wounds. Bathe with a weak solution of antiseptic and allow the patient as much fresh air and exercise as seems sensible. If the dog can lick the wound with his tongue, let him do so as this is the best medicine !

DROWNING. Dogs have been known to fall into wells, vats, or steep-sided pools from which they have been unable to extricate themselves. Still water ponds are particularly dangerous, and swans have been known to deal with medium-sized dogs by

Artificial respiration should be applied when a dog is rescued from a well or pond.
First, remove the victim's collar and hold him up by his hind legs to drain away the water.
Then lie the dog on his side, forelegs foreward, hind legs backwards, and press the flat of both of your hands down on the ribs, then lift sharply. The dog's tongue should be extended from its mouth.

holding them below the surface with one wing. Remove the victim's collar and hold him up by the hind legs for the water to drain away from his body. Apply artificial respiration by lying the dog on his side, his forelegs forward, the hindlegs backward, the flat of the two hands pressing down on his ribs, then lifted sharply. This should be repeated at rhythmic intervals, timed at the rate the dog would normally breathe. The dog's tongue should be kept extended from the mouth while artificial respiration is being applied. An assistant can be usefully employed doing this. When the dog shows signs of breathing, a slight whiff of smelling salts should help, followed by a few drops of *very weak* whisky and water when he is fully conscious and can swallow. Thereafter he should be kept warm and allowed to rest.

ECZEMA. This is a dry condition of the skin which usually starts with bare patches then becomes pustular. There is a discharge which encrusts and causes the dog severe discomfort. A number of effective antibiotic preparations are available, most of them obtainable from the average pet store. It is best to enquire for the latest form of medicine to deal with this unpleasant condition, which if ignored can spread over the dog's body.

GASTRO-ENTERITIS. The usual symptom is a very loose pungent motion which if allowed to continue could well include blood. The first thing is to deal with the diarrhoea, so take the patient off meat at once and give milky foods. The dog will frequently suffer stomach pain and vomit a frothy, white fluid, but the condition will usually mend once the motions have been made firmer. As with all bowel upsets, the veterinary surgeon should be consulted.

HEAT or SUN STROKE. The dog most likely to get this is one who has been thoughtlessly left in his owner's closed car on a hot summer's day. This ill-treated animal should be given a short drink of cool water to which a little salt has been added. His body should then be bathed gently with cold water and he should be allowed to rest and sleep in a shady spot and remain undisturbed.

HERNIAS. The commonest hernia is the umbilical form which is usually seen as a bump on the navel. It is usually caused by an inexperienced dam agitatedly pulling on the cord when the puppy is born and perhaps biting it off roughly so that a rupture is caused. A bitch with an undershot jaw, i.e. with the mouth formed like that of a Bulldog, is very liable to cause this condition because she cannot make a clean bite. Such a rupture need not worry you as it has no adverse effect on the puppy, whether male or female, either now or in later life. If the bump is a large one and unsightly it can be dealt with competently by any veterinary surgeon. It is not an unsoundness, but there are other forms of hernia which are – the Inguinal Hernia, sometimes found in the bitch's groin, also the Diaphragmatic Hernia, the latter being a serious form often caused by an accident.

HYSTERIA. This is a condition often experienced in a dog who has had Distemper. It can occur in a dog confined for long periods in a kennel or room without other company. Most animals get over these distressing bouts quite quickly and the owner should ensure that the dog is reassured and generally fussed and comforted. A quiet dark room where there are no objects likely to injure him is the best place to put a dog having an attack of hysteria.

MANGE. Eczema is one form which has been dealt with earlier. There is also Sarcoptic Mange, a bareness which appears initially on head and ears, also the underparts in the region of belly and groin. Proprietary mange cures can be used with good effect and there are special baths available, although these should be used as a last resort as in certain instances they have been known to have an adverse psychological effect on the dog if applied too frequently.

Follicular Mange is a more serious form of mange. Unfortunately, not too much is known about it and although it is less irritating to the dog it persists and takes a long time to disperse. There are a number of good remedies on the market and in some cases injections are recommended, but your veterinary surgeon will advise how to proceed. In any case, once a cure has been effected, everything the dog had – his bedding, toys etc. should be disposed of and replaced. Even the surrounding area of his sleeping quarters should be thoroughly fumigated and disinfected.

MONORCHIDISM (and Cryptorchidism). These are genital abnormalities in the male dog. A monorchid is one in which only one testicle has descended into the scrotum. Such an animal may have been born with only one, but many have the second testicle retained in the abdomen. A cryptorchid is a dog with neither testicle descended into the scrotum. He may have none, or both may be retained in the abdomen. The condition is said to be hereditary, but it has been corrected in certain instances by the judicious use of hormones. Some breeders consider it unwise to include dogs with these afflictions in their breeding programmes, for if indeed it is hereditary the condition is liable to be passed on to subsequent generations.

PANTING. Young dogs especially will stay out too long in strong direct sunshine and become over-heated. Unless an animal has some shelter which he can retire to when too hot he should not remain in an unprotected position for much more than ten minutes at a time. Dogs perspire through their tongues and are inclined to lose their body fluid with panting much more quickly than humans. Cool water should be available to drink at all times especially in hot weather. A dog which pants persistently should be given a cool, darkened place to rest in until the panting stops.

POISONS. Should your dog be unfortunate enough to have taken poison, the first thing to do is to give an emetic. There are many kinds of poisons, some slow acting others speedy in their effect. Much depends on the amount of poison taken and the main exercise is to cause the dog to vomit as much as possible. The most effective emetics are (a) a dessertspoonful of salt in half a tumbler of warm water (b) a similar solution of mustard and (c) a marble-sized lump of common soda. Should the victim have vomited the contents of his stomach then you can give him the whites of eggs in milk. Try to ascertain what poison has been ingested. The commonest accidents are caused by a dog taking in rat poison, drain cleaners, mole bait, some paints, insect and plant sprays. Usually the containers in which these things are sold reveal the chemicals used in their manufacture, sometimes giving an antidote to use in case of an accident. If you are uncertain as to which poison your dog is suffering from, telephone your veterinary surgeon at once giving him details. He will then tell you how to proceed pending his early arrival. In the meantime keep the dog quiet and reassure him as much as you can.

RESTRAINT. A dog in pain or frightened as the result of an accident may become difficult and dangerous to approach. Even one's own pet in such circumstances can prove wild and vicious and require very firm handling if you are to avoid getting bitten. Get as close as possible to the dog, talking to him all the time. It is best to have a muzzle ready and the best form of this is a 2 in. strip of bandage or cloth about a yard long. Make a loop about midway and slip it over the dog's muzzle, drawing it tight with the knot under the jaws. Then take the loose ends back behind the ears and tie them firmly behind his neck. This will prevent him biting you and allow physical examination. If he continues to struggle it may be necessary to hobble him by tying his forelegs together, also his hindlegs. A dog tied in this manner is prevented from damaging himself and others.

SHOCK. After an accident a dog will suffer from shock. This is usual when a head injury has been sustained or when internal damage has occurred. The symptoms may be seen in the lips and gums which are often pallid when internal bleeding is taking place. Respiration and pulse symptoms vary according to the dog's state and he may show great thirst. If the accident is in an awkward location the dog should be removed from the scene until the veterinary surgeon can examine him. He should be 'eased' on to a blanket and put somewhere quiet. He must be kept warm and allowed to rest until treated.

SHOCK. (Electric). Always keep dogs and exposed electric wires and plugs apart. A dog's instinct is to chew, and flex seems to have a particular attraction. 'Live' wires of this kind and uncovered wall plugs which can be licked are frequently lethal. At best a dog could receive a shock which render him unconscious and burn his mouth. In such accidents a dog often urinates. The first thing to do is to switch off the current: if for some reason you cannot do this push away the wire from the dog's mouth by using any non-conductor, such as a wooden stick. If the animal is unconscious give artificial respiration and treat for shock. The veterinary surgeon should be called in, especially if mouth burns have resulted from the accident.

SPAYING. This is the term given to the operation which prevents a bitch from having puppies. A spayed bitch will not have her usual menstrual period or season, and the male dog will not show an interest in her because of this. You cannot enter a spayed bitch in any dog show run under Kennel Club rules and regulations. On the other hand if these disadvantages are of no importance to you, such a bitch can settle down well in the family circle and give no trouble. The best time to spay is prior to her expected first season, which is usually at about six months of age. However, the operation can be done at any time; the owner remembering that the bitch should be allowed at least a fortnight for the wound to heal. There is a danger that a spayed bitch will run to early fat and over-glossiness. This need not be so if the animal is properly fed and exercised.

SPLINTERS. Sometimes dogs will pick up wood or pine splinters in their pads, or in fact anywhere in their bodies. Once located, the dog should be muzzled to prevent his biting, and the offending splinter extracted with the aid of tweezers. The tweezers should be pushed well down on to the flesh in order to grasp as much of the splinter as possible. Once out, the wound should be dabbed with a little antiseptic.

STINGS. Over-curious dogs often get stung by bees or wasps. The long-coated dog seldom gets stung about his body, but heads, noses, eyes, ears, and lips are vulnerable. Pain and swelling will result and the sting should be extracted with the use of tweezers as soon as possible: the sting mark can then be dressed with antiseptic.

THERMOMETER. A snub-nosed clinical thermometer, rectal type, should be in every dog-owner's medicine chest. To use, cleanse thoroughly in tepid water and shake down the mercury into the bulb. The bulb should then be lightly greased with olive oil and the end inserted gently about two inches into the dog's rectum. The dog should be lying on his side and it is usually best to have someone to help you in this exercise by holding the dog down. Leave the thermometer in place for approximately two minutes. A dog's normal temperature is 38.4°C. The temperature should be determined when the animal has been quiet and not exerted in any way. A significant rise in temperature should be a warning signal that infection may be present. A recorded temperature of 37°C is also abnormal and may indicate shock or near collapse.

WOUNDS. Cut away the hair from the wound area and clean with warm water into which a few drops of antiseptic have been added. If you have none, use salt or Epsom salts in the water. If a foreign object is in the wound remove it with tweezers or forceps. Bandage the area initially; later the dog himself, providing he can reach the wound, will hasten the healing process by licking it.

Giving medicine

Some care should be taken in the administration of medicine to a dog to avoid causing choking and nausea. In effect, you should not open his mouth and pour down the medicine, but observe the following rules:

LIQUIDS: Small dogs are easily handled on one's lap, but it is best to back a large animal into a corner or against a wall. Another method is to get him into a seated position and straddle him with your knees. It is easier if you have an assistant, but failing one, tilt back the dog's head and without opening his mouth slide your index finger down the side of his mouth inside the lips and pull the lips out to make a pouch or pocket. Then pour the liquid medicine into the pouch slowly, and in small doses, giving him ample time to swallow.

PILLS: If the dog is taking food in the normal way there is not much problem; just secrete the pill in a lump of meat or tasty food and it will usually go down unnoticed. If not, coat the pill with honey or butter, open the dog's mouth and put it on the back of tongue and push it down. Close his muzzle with one hand and rub the throat with a downward motion. If he tries to reject it, place the palm of your hand over his nostrils for a second – this will usually dispose of the pill as required.

POWDERS: These usually come in waxed squares of paper. If not, put the powder onto a small square which has been creased down the middle. Open the dog's mouth and deposit the contents on to the back of his tongue by channelling it swiftly down the crease. Massage the throat downwards until the powder has disappeared. Some tasteless powders can be dealt with in the same way as pills by concealing them in food or making a special paste of them with honey or jam.

INHALENTS: In the case of chest colds, bronchitis, and pneumonia it may be necessary to apply some form of inhalent. A 'bronchitis kennel' is made by putting the patient into a closed tea-chest or large dog basket where it cannot get out. The extended spout of a kettle is entered into the box so that the vapour is concentrated within and the dog is forced to inhale it. A suitable vapour can be made by dropping a little Friars Balsam or Eucalyptus into the water. The treatment should be given at intervals of four hours daily, each session lasting for not much more than ten minutes at a time. Great care should be taken to avoid scalding and treatment should not be continued if the dog shows signs of acute distress or fear.

Index

Distributors for
Bartholomew Pet Books

Australia

Book Trade : Tudor Distributors Pty. Limited, 14 Mars Road,
Lane Cove 2066, New South Wales, Australia

Canada

Pet Trade :   Burgham Sales Ltd., 558 McNicoll Avenue,
Willowdale (Toronto), Ontario, Canada M2H 2E1
Book Trade : Clarke Irwin and Company, Limited,
791 St. Clair Avenue W., Toronto, Canada M6C 1B8

New Zealand

Pet Trade :   Masterpet Products Limited,
7 Kaiwharawhara Road, Wellington, New Zealand
Book Trade : Whitcoulls Limited, Trade Department, Private Bag,
Auckland, Wellington, or Christchurch, New Zealand

South Africa

Book Trade : McGraw-Hill Book Company (S.A.) (Pty.) Limited,
P.O. Box 23423, Joubert Park, Johannesburg,
South Africa

U.S.A.

Pet Trade :   Pet Supply Imports Inc., P.O. Box 497, Chicago,
Illinois, U.S.A.
Book Trade : The Two Continents Publishing Group Limited,
30 East 42nd Street, New York, N.Y. 10017, U.S.A.